Quality and Performance Excellence in Higher Education

Quality and Performance Excellence in Higher Education

Baldrige on Campus

Charles W. Sorensen
Julie A. Furst-Bowe
Diane M. Moen

University of Wisconsin–Stout

Editors

ANKER PUBLISHING COMPANY, INC.
Bolton, Massachusetts

Quality and Performance Excellence in Higher Education
Baldrige on Campus

ISBN 1-882982-80-0

Composition by Beverly Jorgensen, Studio J Graphic Design
Cover design by Dutton & Sherman Design

Anker Publishing Company, Inc.
563 Main Street
P.O. Box 249
Bolton, MA 01740-0249 USA

www.ankerpub.com

Library of Congress Cataloging-in-Publication Data

Quality and performance excellence in higher education : Baldrige on campus
/ Charles W. Sorensen, Julie A. Furst-Bowe, Diane M. Moen, editors.
    p. cm.
Includes bibliographical references and index.
  ISBN 1-882982-80-0
   1. Universities and colleges—United States—Administration—Case studies.
2. Total quality management in higher education—United States—Case
studies. 3. Malcolm Baldrige National Quality Award. I. Sorensen, Charles
W. (Charles William), 1941- II. Furst-Bowe, Julie A. III. Moen, Diane M.
LB2341.Q34 2005
  378.1'01—dc22   2004021398

Dedication

This book is dedicated to the students, faculty, staff, and alumni of the University of Wisconsin–Stout. Without their efforts and commitment to excellence, this book would not be possible.

A special thanks to Jan Jordan and Marian Smith for their assistance in preparing this manuscript.

The Editors

Charles W. Sorensen
Chancellor, University of Wisconsin–Stout
Phone: 715-232-2441
Email: sorensenc@uwstout.edu

Charles W. Sorensen is chancellor of the University of Wisconsin–Stout (UW–Stout). Before his appointment in 1988, he served as a member of the faculty and dean of the College of Arts and Sciences at Grand Valley State University and as academic vice president at Winona State University. He has been a strong advocate of partnerships with the private sector and building alliances with K–12 schools. Under his leadership, UW–Stout developed a technology park and an award-winning technology transfer program. He has served on statewide committees and a blue ribbon commission on the future of the state's economy. Dr. Sorensen has been a strong advocate for distance education, developing a digital campus at UW–Stout, private fundraising, and using quality tools in an educational environment. He earned a B.A. from Augustana College, an M.S. from Illinois State University, and a Ph.D. (history) from Michigan State University.

Julie A. Furst-Bowe
Assistant Chancellor, Assessment and Continuous
    Improvement, University of Wisconsin–Stout
Phone: 715-232-5901
Email: furst-bowej@uwstout.edu

Julie A. Furst-Bowe has been in the field of higher education for nearly 20 years. She has been at the

University of Wisconsin–Stout (UW–Stout) since 1990, and served as a faculty member, graduate program director, department chair, and associate vice chancellor for academic and student affairs prior to assuming her current position in 2003. She has been extensively involved with Baldrige efforts at UW–Stout, and serves as an examiner for the Malcolm Baldrige National Quality Award program and as a facilitator for the Academic Quality Improvement Program. She has presented nationally and internationally on quality improvement in higher education, and has consulted with numerous institutions. She currently serves on the board of directors for the Wisconsin Forward Award and as a judge for the Minnesota state quality awards program. She holds a doctorate in education from the University of Minnesota and a master's degree in instructional technology. More information is available at her web site: http://www.uwstout.edu/mba.

Diane M. Moen
Vice Chancellor, Administrative and Student Life
    Services, University of Wisconsin–Stout
Phone: 715-232-1683
Email: moend@uwstout.edu

Diane M. Moen is vice chancellor of administrative and student life services at the University of Wisconsin–Stout (UW–Stout). She began her career at UW–Stout in 1978 and has held several positions including budget analyst, controller, and assistant chancellor. She is active in professional organizations, including the Central Association of College and University Business Officers, and also serves as an executive council member for the National Consortium for Continuous Improvement in Higher Education. She received a B.S. in business administration and an M.B.A from the University of Wisconsin–Eau Claire.

The Contributors

Rick S. Blackburn
New Mexico State University–Carlsbad
Phone: 505-234-9214
Email: rblackburn@cavern.nmsu.edu

Rick S. Blackburn is the campus academic officer at New Mexico State University–Carlsbad. Under his direction, the campus earned three successive Quality New Mexico state quality recognitions, three consecutive awards under the Green Zia Environmental Excellence Program of the New Mexico Department of Environment, and recognition by the National Wildlife Federation as one of the top 20 environmentally friendly schools in the United States. Dr. Blackburn is a past president of the Community College Academic Officers of New Mexico, a past board member of the National Council of Instructional Administrators, a consultant-evaluator for the Higher Learning Commission of the North Central Association of Colleges and Schools, and serves on the board of directors of Quality New Mexico.

Jerrilyn A. Brewer
Western Wisconsin Technical College
Phone: 608-785-9877
Email: BrewerJ@wwtc.edu

Jerrilyn A. Brewer presently serves as associate vice president for strategic effectiveness at Western Wisconsin Technical College (WWTC). She is a senior examiner for the Malcolm Baldrige National Quality Award and a consultant-evaluator for the Higher Learning Commission of the North Central Association. She also facilitates workshops for the Academic Quality Improvement Program (AQIP) of the Higher Learning Commission. She provided the primary leadership for the college's state and national quality award applications. In addition, WWTC is one of the first six higher education institutions to participate in the Higher Learning Commission's AQIP process. Dr. Brewer also works independently with colleges to facilitate strategic planning, assessment, and organizational development initiatives. She received her doctorate in education from the University of Minnesota.

A. Cathleen Greiner
National University
Phone: 858-642-8106
Email: cgreiner@nu.edu

A. Cathleen Greiner is provost and vice president for academic affairs at National University. She has had a long career in higher education with expertise in leadership, administration and management, institutional research, assessment and strategic planning, academic policy research and analysis, teaching and coursework, and program review and development. She is published and annually presents at national conferences on such topics as program and academic assessment, accreditation, faculty development, multicampus systems and processes, and adult learning. Dr. Greiner co-chairs the university's Baldrige team and the Council on Quality

Dean L. Hubbard
Northwest Missouri State University
Phone: 660-562-1110
Email: hubbard@mail.nwmissouri.edu

Dean L. Hubbard is president of Northwest Missouri State University. Under his leadership, Northwest has implemented its Culture of Quality plan to improve the quality of all aspects of the institution's operation, especially undergraduate education. Since 1984, Northwest has received two Missouri Quality Awards, the National Association of College and University Business Officers Higher Education Award, and a grant from the Alfred P. Sloan Foundation for quality improvements in activity-based costing. Dr. Hubbard has earned degrees from Stanford University (Ph.D.); Yonsei University, Seoul, Korea (Korean language); and Andrews University (B.A. and M.A.).

David C. Oehler
Northwest Missouri State University
Phone: 660-562-1527
Email: OEHLER@mail.nwmissouri.edu

David C. Oehler is the director of assessment, information, and analysis at Northwest Missouri State University. His responsibilities at Northwest include coordinating the student outcomes assessment program and the design and implementation of a management information system to provide timely, comprehensive, and relevant decision-making information to chairs, directors, deans, and cabinet-level officers. In addition, he assists departments and teams with defining, validating, measuring, and interpreting key performance indicators, monitoring trends in the field of assessment, and adapting best practices to Northwest's processes. He oversees the collecting and tracking of student outcomes assessment measures and the provision of student assistance programs in individual and group tutoring and supplemental instruction. He holds a doctorate in higher education from Iowa State University.

Patricia E. Potter
National University
Phone: 858-642-8114
Email: ppotter@nu.edu

Patricia E. Potter is vice president for regional operations and marketing at National University. She has been involved with quality initiatives at the university since 1996 and co-chairs the Baldrige team and the Council on Quality. She has held numerous executive positions in business development and marketing positions for privately and publicly held companies, and has expertise in leadership, business processes, student/ customer service, program/product design, development and deployment, and operations and logistics. She is published and presents regularly. She was recently appointed to serve on the California Joint Commission to Update the Master Plan for Education, K–16.

Gerald L. Shadwick
Monfort College of Business
University of Northern Colorado
Phone: 970-351-1209
Email: gerald.shadwick@unco.edu

Gerald L. Shadwick came to the Monfort College of Business after 26 years as a chief executive officer and president of banks in Kansas and Colorado. Earlier he served as administrative assistant to U.S. Senator Frank Carlson and legislative assistant to U.S. Congressman Graham Purcell of Texas. He presently serves on the boards of a large regional construction company and a privately held oil company. At Kansas State University (KSU), he has served on the KSU Alumni Association Board of Directors, the KSU Foundation Board of Trustees, and the Dean's Advisory Board of the College of Business Administration. At the Monfort College, he has taught business courses in politics and ethics, management, and business law. Four times he has been selected by students as Professor of the Year, and he earned the Teaching Excellence Award from the faculty. He has been active in initiating Baldrige-type quality management systems in the business college and helped start an undergraduate class in management of quality.

Table of Contents

Foreword

This book is about continuous quality improvement in higher education with a focus on case studies from six very diverse institutions throughout the United States. No other country in the world relies so heavily on its higher education system for its future or bestows so much freedom and choice on its faculty and students. No other country has created so many institutions, of such diversity, in so many different locations. And no other country has enjoyed the prosperity from such an educated population. Education is an investment that pays itself back, both principal and interest, in every generation.

However, higher education in the United States is currently facing many serious challenges, including providing access for an increasing number of students; keeping college affordable for students of all ages and circumstances; using technology effectively in teaching and learning; joining with K–12 schools and other institutions in partnerships that serve society; and fostering economic growth and workforce development. It is extremely difficult to meet these challenges given the current environment of limited financial resources, and it is clear that institutions must reexamine traditional methods of operation in order to remain viable now and in the future.

The six institutions featured in this book have demonstrated an ability to meet these challenges and serve as national role models because they have effectively applied a systematic framework for quality improvement—the Baldrige criteria for performance excellence in education. In fact, the University of Wisconsin–Stout became the first higher education institution to receive the Malcolm Baldrige National Quality Award in 2001.

Quality improvement in higher education is exhilarating and discomforting at the same time because it asks students, faculty, staff, and administrators to think in new ways, to be open to new ideas, and to work together to enhance student learning and organizational performance. Application of the Baldrige criteria requires open communication and collaboration among students, faculty members, support service providers, and administrators, and it succeeds only when all of these stakeholders understand the institutional mission, share a common vision for the future, and are dedicated to reaching institutional goals.

The educational institutions described here have publicly demonstrated their commitment to continuous quality improvement and have been publicly recognized for their efforts. Although these schools have very different missions, each has engaged in rigorous self-assessment and has been open in sharing its strengths, vulnerabilities, and success stories. We should be asking every higher education institution to engage in these practices and focus on how to best serve their students. Each school should be engaged in honest self-assessment and in determining appropriate goals and objectives for student learning, stakeholder fulfillment, resource management, and employee satisfaction. The focus should be on outcomes, results, and accountability to all stakeholders in each of these important areas.

Effective leadership is essential for continuous quality improvement. The schools in this book have top administrators with strong academic values and exceptional communication skills; they are team builders who strategize for an uncertain future. In an era where most college presidents stay in their positions for only five years, many of these individuals have served the same institution for more than a decade, and their unwavering commitment to building high quality, high performing organizations is unmatched among their peers. They were among the first to utilize the Baldrige criteria when these became available to educators in 1999, and have used the Baldrige process to lead their institutions on remarkable quality journeys. For example, in his remarks at the Baldrige awards ceremony in 2002, President George W. Bush commented on the accomplishments of the University of Wisconsin–Stout and observed that this institution was an outstanding role model for 21st century education organizations.

Indeed, a lack of commitment by senior leadership was identified as one of five major barriers to implementing systematic quality improvement in higher education, according to a survey of 160 colleges and universities (Horine & Hailey, 1995). Other barriers included changing organizational culture, gaining faculty support, finding implementation time in already busy schedules, and the cost and time required for staff training. Although the institutions described in this book did not face the problem of uncommitted senior leadership, each did address the remaining barriers in its own unique way.

In each of the chapters, you will see how the schools integrated quality improvement into existing processes, instead of adding quality improvement as a separate or stand-alone initiative. You'll learn how they gained faculty and staff buy-in and ultimately changed organizational culture through open communication channels, employee education and professional development programs, and by involving faculty, staff, and students in meaningful processes and activities. These schools have developed some of the most promising models for student learning and engagement and the use of technology, even as they faced unfavorable budgetary circumstances. They utilize systematic processes to allocate and/or reallocate resources to fund areas of high priority, providing the means to maintain continuous improvement efforts.

Whether the majority of higher education institutions will be able to maintain and advance quality teaching and learning given the many challenges they face in the current environment is an issue of serious concern. Many institutions will muddle through the next decade by making only incremental changes and employing short-term fixes while others may be forced to close their doors (Guskin & Marcy, 2003). The six institutions in this book recognize that long-term problems require long-term solutions and, through use of the Baldrige criteria and processes, have developed a clear vision of the future focused on student learning and performance, employee satisfaction and well-being, stakeholder partnerships, and fiscal responsibility.

This book is written for institutions that are serious about redesigning traditional methods of operation in order to systematically improve teaching and learning, as well as administrative and student support processes. The approaches, strategies, models, and tools of the six award-winning institutions are shared in each chapter. This book is an essential resource for anyone interested in learning how the Baldrige criteria can be successfully applied in a variety of educational settings to achieve performance excellence.

Katharine C. Lyall, President
University of Wisconsin System

References

Guskin, A., & Marcy, M. (2003). Dealing with the future now: Principles for creating a vital campus in a climate of restricted resources. *Change, 13*(4), 10–21.

Horine, J. E., & Hailey, W. A. (1995). Challenges to successful quality management implementation in higher education institutions. *Innovative Higher Education, 20*(1), 7–17.

1

Introduction

It is change, continuing change, inevitable change,
that is the dominant force in society today.
                                        — Isaac Asimov

It is clear from all indicators that both public and private colleges and universities will continue to face severe fiscal issues, more demands from governing boards and state legislatures on efficiencies and accountability measures, and great pressure to hold down the rising cost of education. College and university officials will be forced to find answers or at least explore measures to assure students and stakeholders that they understand and are addressing the issues. Senior administrators, governing board members, and faculty leaders will find this book useful because it suggests a quality improvement model that is proving to be very effective for those who manage educational institutions.

This book reviews six unique colleges and universities—University of Wisconsin–Stout, Monfort College of Business at the University of Northern Colorado, New Mexico State University–Carlsbad, National University, Northwest Missouri State University, Western Wisconsin Technical College—pioneers in the effort to adopt a new, dynamic approach to academic and administrative excellence—the Malcolm Baldrige National Quality Award program. The practice of continuous quality improvement in higher education, the perspective of best practices, and meaningful feedback from students and stakeholders are essential for healthy, vibrant, effective institutions. These colleges and universities are true pioneers because they are challenging well-established assumptions, they are adopting new leadership models, and they are demonstrating that higher education can be more accountable.

The Baldrige framework is an excellent quality model that effectively assesses and measures institutional improvement. The Baldrige criteria for education, first published in 1999, provide a comprehensive structure for educational institutions to align their mission, vision, values, and goals with the resources essential for a long-term improvement effort. The program is both nonprescriptive and comprehensive, and so fits any institution. For more than five years, the Baldrige education criteria have been used by hundreds of United States educational institutions to improve performance (Baldrige National Quality Program, 2004).

Each of the institutions profiled in this book has adopted the Malcolm Baldrige education criteria for performance excellence. The criteria are built upon a set of core values and concepts, which are embedded in the beliefs and behaviors found in high performing organizations. These core values and concepts include visionary leadership; learning-centered education; organizational and personal learning; valuing faculty, staff, and partners; agility; focus on the future; managing for innovation; management by fact; focus on results; and creating value and a systems perspective (Baldrige National Quality Program, 2004).

Malcolm Baldrige National Quality Award Criteria

The core values and concepts are embodied in seven categories.

- **Leadership:** How senior leaders guide the institution and review institutional performance; how the institution is governed; and how the organization addresses its responsibilities to the public, ensures ethical behavior, and supports key communities

- **Strategic planning:** How the strategic planning process addresses key factors; how strategic objectives are established; how action plans are developed and deployed

- **Student, stakeholder, and market focus:** How the institution determines its markets; listens to and learns from students and stakeholders; builds relationships with students and stakeholders; and determines student and stakeholder satisfaction

- **Measurement, analysis, and knowledge management:** How the institution measures, analyzes, and improves student and operational performance information at all levels; how the institution ensures the quality and availability of needed information for faculty, staff, students, and external audiences; and how the institution builds and manages its knowledge assets

- **Faculty and staff focus:** How the institution's work systems enable faculty and staff to achieve high performance; how faculty and staff education, training, and career development support overall institutional objectives and build employee knowledge, skills, and capabilities

- **Process management:** How the institution identifies and manages its key processes for maximizing student learning; and how the institution manages its key processes that support the learning environment

- **Organizational performance results:** Documented results in six key areas including student learning; student and stakeholder satisfaction; financial; faculty and staff performance and satisfaction; organizational effectiveness; and governance and social responsibility

Educational organizations may use these criteria for internal self-assessment, or they may address the criteria in a 50-page application and submit the application for external review, scoring, and award consideration. Each application is evaluated and scored by a team of trained examiners who have backgrounds and expertise in a variety of sectors. High-scoring applications go on to receive a site visit by the examiner team to verify and clarify the information included in the application. Finally, a panel of highly qualified judges selects the award recipients each year. Regardless of how many points an application scores, each applicant receives a comprehensive feedback report detailing key themes as well as organizational strengths and opportunities for improvement in each of the seven categories.

Since the education category was added to the Malcolm Baldrige National Quality Award program in 1999, there have been more than 60 applicants to the program and four award winners—three public schools or school districts in Alaska, Illinois, and New York, and the University of Wisconsin–Stout (UW–Stout), which became the first postsecondary recipient in 2001. In addition to the Malcolm Baldrige National Quality Award program, 40 states have similar quality award programs based on the Baldrige criteria and application evaluation processes. Each of the institutions in this volume has been recognized at the state or national level for its quality improvement efforts.

Institutional Accreditation

The value of the Baldrige framework has influenced change in schools, school districts, community colleges, and universities for the past several years. In addition, the framework has begun to have a significant influence on the approaches used by regional accrediting associations (Ruben, 2004). For example, the concept of quality enhancement is at the heart of the Southern Association of Colleges and Schools Commission on Colleges' philosophy of accreditation (www.sacscoc.org). Each institution applying for accreditation or renewal of accreditation is required to develop a Quality Enhancement Plan. Engaging the wider academic community and addressing one or more issues that contribute to institutional improvement, the plan must be focused and succinct. The Quality Enhancement Plan describes a carefully designed and focused course of action that addresses a well-defined topic or key issue(s) related to enhancing student learning and performance.

The Higher Learning Commission of the North Central Association of Colleges and Schools has developed and implemented an alternative accreditation process that supports institutions using continuous improvement systems (Spangehl, 2004). This process, named the Academic Quality Improvement Program (AQIP), shifts the focus of accreditation from inputs—such as SAT scores, faculty credentials, or number of library volumes—to performance, or how well an institution meets the long-term needs of its students and stakeholders (Spanghel, 2004). Presently, more than 100 postsecondary institutions have selected this method of accreditation including three of the institutions included in this book:

UW–Stout, Western Wisconsin Technical College, and New Mexico State University–Carlsbad. A complete list of AQIP participants can be found on the AQIP web site, http://www.AQIP.org.

To restructure accreditation, AQIP did not simply substitute a set of output indices for the traditional input requirements. Instead, it followed the Baldrige approach of delineating organizational subsystems, or groups of processes, that strive for related goals, and asking institutions to identify their own performance measures within each of these subsystems (Spanghel, 2004). Like Baldrige, AQIP is a nonprescriptive approach that keeps the institution focused on improving performance. AQIP allows institutions that have embraced continuous quality improvement to incorporate accreditation into their everyday operations and activities.

In addition to the regional accrediting organizations, many program-specific accrediting bodies (e.g., Accreditation Board for Engineering and Technology and the National Council for Accreditation of Teacher Education) are moving in the direction of an outcomes-based, continuous review process rather than the traditional periodic assessment to ensure a university's or college's ability to achieve its mission.

Approaches to Baldridge Deployment

The institutions featured in this book are champions of quality improvement and have embraced the Baldrige framework as a method of continuous improvement. Two universities—Northwest Missouri State and UW–Stout—represent two rather distinct approaches to the Baldrige process. Northwest Missouri State has been engaged in the process of quality improvement since 1991 and has been recognized twice by the Missouri Quality Award. At Northwest, the Baldrige process penetrates the structure very deeply. The university has used two approaches: Career Pathing and the Seven-Step Planning Process. The former focuses on faculty and staff and includes coaching and mentoring, assisting individuals to achieve personal and organizational goals; the latter focuses on systematic process improvement. The Seven-Step Planning Process, deployed at the department level, is integral to developing and delivering all new educational programs or student services processes. It requires that virtually everyone at the university understands and is involved in the Northwest Quality Systems Model.

UW–Stout adopted the Baldrige model as an overarching program, a system that unifies the campus without requiring standardization across all campus units. While planning at the divisional and departmental levels must align with the vision, mission, and short- and long-term goals of the campus, there is room for variation in planning and deployment. The university does not require, for example, that faculty members adopt Baldrige processes for the classroom. Yet the campus provides extensive faculty development opportunities to improve teaching and learning. Metrics that reflect classroom performance, including assessment of student learning, placement rates, and employer satisfaction with graduates, are benchmarked nationally against peer institutions. These metrics compare very favorably against other institutions, and some, including employer satisfaction, are considered best in class.

UW–Stout focuses on broader, all-university systems and functions that drive the program. Significant structural changes made in the mid-1990s, including an inclusive Chancellor's Advisory Council; an Office of Budget, Planning, and Analysis; and an open, participatory budget process, are strategies that effectively deploy the Baldrige criteria and core values. Quality initiatives are driven by the strong leadership system and, in effect, trickle down to all units on campus.

Thus, two quite different universities adopted different philosophies in implementing the Baldrige model, and each works well within its respective culture. The following section highlights how the dissimilar colleges and universities featured in this book approach five core components of the Baldrige model and some of the themes common to each.

Leadership

Since each college or university is unique in its own right, each has a slightly different definition or approach to how leaders, or the leadership system, address values and performance expectations, or deal with governance, students, and the various categories of stakeholders. Yet, each embraces the common theme of distributed, integrated, or shared systems of leadership. Western Wisconsin Technical College, for example, identifies the president, the three vice presidents and associate vice president, and a director as the senior leadership team. A committee representing senior leaders, union members, faculty, and students serves as a steering group that is integral to collaborative decision-making. Teams are connected through the district board, the Senior Leadership Team, and the Steering and Implementation Teams. This dynamic process assures strong communication with all groups; alignment with the mission, vision, and values of the institution; and guarantees that all decisions reflect the school's four strategic priorities—enrollment, retention, learning, and satisfaction.

At the Monfort College of Business at the University of Northern Colorado, the dean, the associate and assistant deans, and the Administrative Council (faculty representatives) represent the senior leaders. Working through a shared governance system, the leadership establishes short- and long-term directions for the college, deploys the values, and establishes performance expectations. The Administrative Council assumes strong and direct communication with the faculty of the college. This process also ensures a close alignment among the vision, mission, and budget expenditures. Key performance indicators are reviewed by the senior leaders, faculty committees, the Administrative Council, and the dean, and are utilized, when appropriate, to make program changes to improve performance.

This collaborative planning strategy at Monfort resulted in a dramatic shift for the college. Its mission changed from a comprehensive school of business with degrees offered through the doctorate, to a new mission focusing only on delivering "high quality, undergraduate-only business education," with the goal of achieving accreditation from the Association to Advance Collegiate Schools of Business. The college realized its accreditation goal by eliminating graduate programs and paring down its educational degrees to the B.S. in business administration.

New Mexico State University–Carlsbad (NMSU–C) deploys a leadership system that is highly collaborative. NMSU–C is a two-year branch campus of New Mexico State University–Las Cruces, a land-grant university. The branch campus is an open admissions community college that accepts any applicant who wishes to attend. The Campus Executive Committee (CEC) consists of the campus executive officer, the campus academic officer, the campus student services officer, and the campus finance officer. This group, assisted by midlevel committees, provides direction for planning, assessment, fiscal management, and resource allocations. The four officers deploy the mission, core values, and performance expectations in their respective areas.

Seven standing committees, representing the functional areas of the campus, consist of members of the faculty, the classified staff, the administration, the student body, and one member from CEC. A steering committee representing one member from each of the standing committees meets on a regular basis and ensures that the entire campus has a voice in all decisions made. Senior leaders actively adopt and review assessment tools, feedback from surveys, state and national reports on adult basic education programs, Perkins grant activities, Title V programs, and Quality New Mexico applications. This information is shared widely, and from the analysis of this information, goals and strategies are developed or revised and integrated into a strategy for improvement.

Communication

A critical part of a healthy organization is clear, effective communication. This means far more than just providing information on issues or on the vision and mission of the institution. It requires active participation; it demands openness on the part of individuals at all levels; and it requires that everyone has an opportunity to be heard, to discuss the issues, and to have a role in decisions before they are finalized. Respected authors (Reina & Reina, 1999) label this as trust communication when information is openly and truthfully shared, when mistakes can be admitted, and when there is open, constructive dialogue on all issues within an organization.

UW–Stout places great emphasis on communication. The variety of approaches used include annual facilitated group discussions to hear from faculty, staff, and students on what they consider as emerging issues; specific forums for the three governance groups on campus; and meetings with individual departments. All budget information, minutes from the bimonthly meetings of the Chancellor's Advisory Council, results of hearings on emerging issues for the university, and outcomes from the annual retreat to identify short-term priorities are shared on the university web site. A monthly email from the chancellor keeps everyone abreast of university issues, as well as University of Wisconsin System and/or statewide issues that may affect the campus. A great variety of listening posts exists that represent the university's efforts, including annual employee satisfaction surveys and annual student satisfaction and engagement surveys.

Technology is used very effectively to enhance communication at Western Wisconsin Technical College. WIRE—a special intranet web site for employees—allows easy access to college policies and forms, departmental web sites, and state information from state web sites. Various stakeholders, including the District Board Community Employers, K–12 schools and districts, have available access to virtually all information from the college web site. Students seeking information about available services or online courses can also use the web site. A robust ITV and video conferencing capability permits classes to be shared with other campuses and provides counseling for students in remote areas. In addition to the effective use of technology to encourage understanding issues, solicitation of feedback is also employed. Budget forums are held to inform employees and listen to individual concerns. Union/management forums are also offered, particularly prior to a ratification vote for a new contract. Teams of faculty and staff have been an effective communication tool to connect the campus with the local governing board as well as to campus leaders.

The Monfort College of Business has a sharp focus on open communication, sharing information widely, and shared decision-making. An Administrative Council consisting principally of faculty serves as a direct conduit between the academic chairs, departmental faculty, and the dean of the college (the senior administrator for the organization). Faculty meetings, individual meetings with faculty members, and email exchanges focus on all-college issues and provide effective feedback to the Administrative Council. As a very student-centered college, a strong emphasis is placed on formal communication with the student body; again, electronic media is used extensively. A number of programs reach out to external stakeholders, such as leadership programs, students serving as consultants for small businesses, and encouraging student involvement in such activities as Junior Achievement.

Quality Tools

Another key component of the Baldrige model is that it is nonprescriptive, allowing each institution to select quality tools and performance indicators that reflect its unique mission and vision. Northwest Missouri State University, for example, uses "dashboard" as a tracking tool for senior administrators to determine performance metrics relative to targets in real time.

Dashboard information is widely shared and aggregated through databases and spreadsheets to track university-wide data. Western Wisconsin Technical College adopted the "WWTC scorecard" to review college-level strategic priorities (enrollment, retention, learning and satisfaction) on a five-year cycle. A program scorecard has also been adopted to review the college's academic programs against statewide data.

All of the schools in the study use local surveys, national surveys, and benchmarking surveys as part of the continuous improvement program. Monfort College assesses its strategic objectives in five areas: program quality, curriculum, faculty, students, and technology. Within each category, best-in-class benchmarks are established, national surveys are used to determine the school's performance, and target stretch goals are established. At UW–Stout, a variety of internal and external surveys are used, ranging from the National Survey of Student Engagement and the ACT Student Opinion Survey to internal surveys. The university relies on survey responses from employer satisfaction with graduates, job placement, and alumni satisfaction. To assess alumni satisfaction with academic programs, National University, the only private institution included in this book, conducts an annual survey of all graduates. The results of that survey are used to determine whether course or program delivery should be modified. National University monitors its key performance measures carefully and frequently using the dashboard quality tool. This is shared with the senior executive team. In addition, extensive use of the feedback from the Baldrige application, student comments on programs, alumni surveys, employer surveys, and stakeholder feedback provide data on satisfaction with programs and services.

Faculty and Staff Focus

Each institution must address the general issue of human resources and, within that, how the organization provides professional development training, succession planning, and a generally healthy work environment. Again, the institutions in this study all address the matter in slightly different ways, depending on the institution and any restrictions at the board or state level. Northwest Missouri State has a strong, systematic succession planning process in place, approved by the board of regents. A select pool of faculty and staff are identified to participate in a mentoring program. When vacancies occur in leadership positions, those individuals can then be considered. One-half of the present leadership team members were internal appointments. UW–Stout is discouraged from such planning by a strong, statewide affirmative action process that requires open searches for all vacancies, although leadership training is provided to employees through several formal development programs. Monfort College shares a similar situation, although several leadership positions have been filled by internal candidates.

At least five of the institutions have very active and successful human resource development programs in place for both faculty and staff, including support staff. At Western Wisconsin Technical College, new employees attend two days of orientation: one is a general program, and the second is a training session, "Becoming a Great College," which focuses on the quality effort of the institution. An Employee Success Policy was implemented to assist employees in succeeding within their particular jobs, not simply assessing performance. Northwest Missouri State has adopted the "Disney way" of thoroughly introducing new employees to the culture of the university and the quality effort. UW–Stout implemented a very successful yearlong leadership program for staff that includes a team project relating to the goals and objectives of the university. NMSU–C provides technical training in such areas as web site design, database applications, and on- and off-campus training sessions.

National University has a unique and well-developed faculty development plan. No tenure system is in place, but there is a systematic incentive plan for faculty that reinforces their critical role for the university. All individuals hired have appropriate skills and experience, and the performance-based environment provides supervisors the opportunity to work with each member of the faculty on annual goals and objectives. University-supported programs allow for upgrading skills, opportunities for annual merit increases, and, if a person's performance is superior, the chance to be recognized with a President's Player Award. Some staff members are students who are working as paid internal interns—students who are employed in various positions on campus as they complete their degrees. The purpose is to provide these students with skills in a business environment. Most of the interns leave after graduating from National and take positions in the private sector.

Strategic Planning

Strategic planning is central to any successful organization since it describes the future direction of an institution. In a sense, it embraces and articulates a vision, and strategies to achieve that vision. Each of the institutions included has well-thought-out, well-developed strategic plans reflecting the uniqueness of each and balancing both short- and long-term goals.

In developing its strategic plan (NU 2005), National University identifies strategic directions. From these goals, strategic objectives are developed and serve as the supporting and coordinating framework for all planning activities. The plan remains flexible, recognizing that internal or external change can happen quickly, requiring an agile, adaptable response. Strategic directions and objectives are not set in stone, but are driven by core themes and values that are carefully analyzed on an annual basis, permitting operating units to gather, analyze, and interpret data and implement essential changes. Change is measured by describing what took place, providing evidence of change and internal or external validation. The budget process, for example, could support issues outside of the strategic plan if an issue emerged after the planning document was complete.

NMSU–C and Western Wisconsin Technical College plan for specific issues. NMSU–C drives its planning process around a five-year plan, a three-year technology plan, a marketing plan, a student retention plan, and a plan for upgrading the physical plant. This focus on critical issues directs a campus plan appropriate to mission, vision, and core values and includes divisional plans and multiyear data projections. With critical feedback from students, stakeholders, and other relevant data review, the Campus Executive Committee identifies specific three- and five-year development plans. Action steps emerge from this process and trigger annual budget decisions. Western Wisconsin Technical College's strategic five-year plan focuses on five key operational areas: facilities, technology, instruction, enrollment, and retention. A Strategic Priorities Plan is developed, strategic challenges are identified, and an annual budget process serves as a guide for division- and unit-level action plans.

UW–Stout focuses sharply on alignment of mission, vision, short- and long-term goals and objectives, and the budget process. This is accomplished by a simple yet effective strategic planning process that rests on a completely participative approach with open communication that is data driven and outcome based. Three groups are integral to the process: 1) the Chancellor's Advisory Council, which aligns planning with resource allocation; 2) the formal Strategic Planning Committee, which develops and reviews mission, vision, and values statements; and 3) the Office of Budget, Planning, and Analysis, which provides institutional research, fiscal analysis, and budget modeling; develops the annual budget process; and drives the capital plan. Since 1996, over 45 budget priorities have been funded.

Northwest Missouri State University's sophisticated planning process includes strategic planning teams; review of external environmental scans; state, national, and global data; and "megatrend" statements developed and used by the Strategic Planning Council. An internal analysis is also conducted and shared with the council. Strategic initiatives are developed in the next stage of planning and "champions" are assigned to oversee each initiative. The initiatives are implemented at a department or unit level through a well-developed and thorough Seven-Step Planning Process; a process that requires each unit to identify action plans, assess and track performance, identify improvement priorities, and set stretch goals.

Conclusion

While this short review has offered a brief glance at how these innovative, creative institutions are addressing change, the following chapters provide rich, insightful detail on the implementation and deployment of the Baldrige model. Each school is different, yet the model is effective because it is mission driven—each institution uses it uniquely. It is also comprehensive; thus, all aspects of a college or university can be examined and processes deployed to ensure that effective measures of continuous improvement are in place.

Even as all of the schools use the Baldrige model to promote effective change, UW–Stout has witnessed dramatic results. In the mid-1990s, it was a university in crisis. A dramatic budget reduction resulted in a great deal of tension on campus. Communication broke down between faculty and administration, creating a level of distrust on how budget decisions would be handled and whether the administration would be open and honest with governance. In the midst of this, the chancellor, at the request of the University of Wisconsin System, proposed charter status for the university, effectively withdrawing from the system and creating a state-supported, independent university. This idea had not been shared widely. When the chancellor asked for and received permission from the board of regents to study the issue, the campus erupted, resulting in a stinging vote of no confidence in the chancellor's leadership.

In response to this crisis, the UW–Stout administration met frequently with faculty, listened attentively, and worked with faculty leadership to enact major structural changes. The first major change was the formation of the Chancellor's Advisory Council, an inclusive, 21-member council representing every constituent group on campus, including governance. Meeting biweekly, the council creates clear lines of communication with faculty, staff, and students; shares all information; and the chancellor makes no decisions until an issue has been discussed with this group.

A second and significant change resulted in creating the Office of Budget, Planning, and Analysis. This is an independent office that initiates the annual, highly participatory budget process, provides all data analysis, and monitors progress on all short- and long-term priorities.

Appointing a chief information officer and assigning responsibility for all technology planning became the third major change. With dedicated hard work by both faculty and senior administrative leaders, the campus not only returned to normalcy but changed fundamentally. Now relying on open communication, shared decision-making, and data-driven decisions, the campus thrives. UW–Stout traveled the road from crisis to quality, demonstrating that positive, lasting change is possible.

Transformational change is essential because there are deeper, elemental forces that affect virtually every college and university in the country. Market forces will demand further change from the more traditional institutions because there are simply more options for students. For-profit universities, virtual universities, and aggressive and creative private colleges and universities remain much more sensitive to individuals whose needs cannot be met by institutions unwilling to direct programs and program delivery when and where it is convenient for the consumer. In a sense, education has become a commodity, driven by market demand and serving specialized needs.

With few exceptions, these powerful, relentless forces will require institutions to revolutionize, adapt to a new environment, and remain competitive, or they will become much less successful and perhaps even fail. It is imperative that presidents and chancellors, those who provide leadership for the nation's colleges and universities, recognize this, adjust to it, and adopt models of change that work. The Malcolm Baldrige National Quality model is a powerful tool to guide transformational change, as the following chapters demonstrate.

References

Baldrige National Quality Program. (2004). *Education criteria for performance excellence.* Gaithersburg, MD: National Institute for Standards and Technology.

Reina, D. S., & Reina, M. L. (1999). *Trust and betrayal in the workplace.* San Francisco, CA: Berrett-Koehler.

Ruben, B. D. (2004). *Pursuing excellence in higher education: Eight fundamental challenges.* San Francisco, CA: Jossey-Bass.

Spangehl, S. D. (2004). The North Central Association of Colleges and Schools Academic Quality Improvement Project (AQIP). In B. D. Ruben, *Pursuing excellence in higher education: Eight fundamental challenges* (pp. 179–189). San Francisco, CA: Jossey-Bass.

2

University of Wisconsin–Stout

Charles W. Sorensen, Julie A. Furst-Bowe, Diane M. Moen

The University of Wisconsin–Stout (UW–Stout) is one of the 13 publicly supported universities in the University of Wisconsin System. Located 70 miles east of the twin cities of Minneapolis and St. Paul, Minnesota, UW–Stout is designated as a special mission institution, forged from the heritage of its founder, Senator James Huff Stout. Senator Stout, a Wisconsin industrialist, founded the Stout Manual Training School in 1891, with programs centered on industrial arts and home economics. Now, more than 110 years later, UW–Stout's 8,000 students are enrolled in career-oriented programs in areas such as business, engineering, art and design, hotel and restaurant management, and teacher education. UW–Stout began its quality journey in the early 1990s, with the introduction of total quality management concepts and training to its 1,200 employees. In 2001, UW–Stout became the first postsecondary institution to receive the Malcolm Baldrige National Quality Award.

Leadership Systems

Led by Charles W. Sorensen, who has served as chancellor since 1988, UW–Stout is responsible to meet the goals set by the board of regents, oversee day-to-day academic and support operations, and interface with the community and other key stakeholders. On paper, UW–Stout's orga-

17

nization is a set of typical hierarchical university functions. There are two divisions: academic and student affairs, and administrative and student life services, each led by a vice chancellor. A dean leads each school or college, with department chairs and faculty managing academic objectives.

Chapter 36 of the *General Statutes of Wisconsin* requires the formation of additional decision-making functions called shared governance within the faculty, academic staff, and students. These functions have primary responsibility for the formation, development, and review of policies concerning their functions related to academic and educational activities and faculty personnel matters. UW–Stout has three governance bodies: 1) Faculty Senate, 2) Senate of Academic Staff, and 3) Stout Student Association. The concept of shared governance provides equal representation in the decision-making process but complicates the organizational structure and inhibits rapid decision-making. Recognizing these issues, UW–Stout created an innovative new leadership system in 1996.

This leadership system removes the organizational complications and inhibitors, encourages responsive multidirectional communication, and flattens the organization structure through broad involvement of all governance bodies. The Chancellor's Advisory Council (CAC) is the core of the leadership system. It meets biweekly and involves 21 university leaders including administrators, faculty, staff, and students. These members of the senior leadership team provide the communication conduit to and from their organizations, resulting in strong communication linkages, participatory decision-making, and enhanced opportunity for meaningful roles in shared governance matters.

Supporting the CAC are a number of established committees such as the Strategic Planning Committee, the Planning and Review Committee, the Curriculum and Instruction Committee, and the Educational Support Unit Review Committee, among others. These established committees contain cross-campus representation and will typically report to one of the CAC members. These committees also provide additional avenues for the CAC to deploy actions, analyze issues, and provide results and feedback to the CAC.

Leadership Direction and Performance Review

The annual summer CAC retreat plays an essential role in setting the leadership direction of the campus. During the retreat, the mission, vision, and values of the university are reviewed, and current information on past performance, progress on strategic objectives, UW System initiatives, and educational best practices are evaluated by the group. From these evaluations the CAC refines and determines areas in need of improvement, identifies future opportunities, and sets university budget priorities for the next fiscal year. The university budget priorities generated from the summer retreat are further developed, and performance expectations are delineated through a campus-wide participatory process, which is discussed in the strategic planning process section.

The CAC also plays a key role in organizational performance review. This primary leadership team reviews overall organizational performance and progress on university priorities through a series of meetings that lead up to the annual retreat. In addition, specific groups of senior leaders report to the CAC on progress toward key goals during specific time-frames, such as progress toward enrollment goals, projections on budget increases or reductions, and updates on new technology initiatives. Comparative data on all performance indicators are utilized whenever appropriate. The use of comparative data provides the CAC with information to identify performance gaps, ascertain leadership performance, and to evaluate changing trends.

Leadership Development

When the CAC was first established in 1996, representatives from the various administrative units and governance groups were not well informed on the issues facing the campus nor did they know how to work together to achieve common goals. To give the new leadership team the knowledge and skills it needed, the Administrative Leadership Team (ALT) was formed. This group, with composition nearly identical to the CAC, has been meeting regularly for approximately eight years to engage in team building, leadership training and relationship building (see Figure 2.1). Skill building is accomplished through formal team building activities, discussions of current articles, and meetings with chief executive officers.

Figure 2.1

The Administrative Leadership Team at the University of Wisconsin–Stout

---

Vision
Develop and be recognized as a world-class leadership system.

Mission
Function as an effective leadership team.

Goals
Collaborative relationship building: ALT members will value and practice participative and interdependent administration. ALT members will have a general understanding of team theory, quality tools, participate in team-building exercises, enhance communication skills, and respect each member's skills and knowledge.

Professional development: ALT provides an opportunity for skill development in a broad variety of areas related to leadership, administration, management, and the university's strategic plan. ALT encourages the use of these skills throughout the organization.

Emerging issues forum: Members are encouraged to view and be knowledgeable of global, national, state, and local higher education issues. The emerging issue discussion promotes idea exchange and issues management, allows for differences of opinion, and elevates awareness of future change agendas.

In recent years, meeting topics have often focused on quality improvement and have involved off-site visits to share ideas and benchmark in specific areas with manufacturing companies, health care systems, and other Baldrige Award recipients and postsecondary institutions. A subset of the group acts as a steering committee and plans the scheduled meetings in consultation with the chancellor. Each meeting is evaluated and the evaluations are annually reviewed and input obtained on suggestions for future topics and continuous improvement of the leadership team development system. ALT members also improve their individual leadership skills via participation in professional organizations, leadership roles in external organizations, and developmental seminars.

Senior leaders—including the chancellor, vice chancellors, and deans—are evaluated by faculty and staff through a comprehensive survey on a periodic basis. The results of the evaluations are shared widely across the campus. These evaluations, along with direct feedback received through numerous listening and learning methods, are used to improve the performance of individual leaders and the leadership system.

Support of Key Communities

UW–Stout has extensive involvement and organizational partnering initiatives to actively support and strengthen local, regional, state, national, professional, and community groups. To ensure key community initiatives are identified and prioritized and actions are aligned to UW–Stout's long-term goals, community involvement and economic development initiatives are integrated into UW-Stout's strategic and budget planning process and are part of its strategic objectives.

UW–Stout's senior leaders, faculty, and staff promote the community's education and economic health. The senior leadership team lead by example through their involvement in such UW–Stout affiliates as the Stout Technology Park, the Stout Technology Transfer Institute, and the Stout Foundation, as well as through their leadership roles in community organizations, including the Menomonie Development Committee, Momentum Chippewa Valley, and the Menomonie Area Chamber of Commerce. Through the chancellor's leadership in the Stout Technology Park, at least 1,000 new high-paying jobs have been added to the region.

Faculty and staff have extensive community involvement, with participation on school boards, city council, nonprofit boards, and other local, state, and national associations and professional societies. Senior leaders also support quality initiatives in higher education by giving numerous Baldrige-related presentations and workshops nationally and internationally, sharing their experiences with other academic institutions, contributing to publications, serving as Baldrige examiners, and through leadership in state quality awards programs.

Strategic Planning

UW–Stout's strategic planning process builds upon the structure of the leadership system and incorporates the university's values of participation, communication, and data-driven, outcome-based results. The process has six intended outcomes:

- Facilitate planning and discussion

- Encourage participation

- Improve the quality of decisions and buy-in

- Build a trusting climate

- Increase understanding of plan and budget

- Strategically focus the campus

The strategic planning process includes the development of mission, vision, and values statements (see Figure 2.2). It incorporates situational analysis, including stakeholder visioning. Goal statements require the deployment of action plans and periodic reviews to monitor and alter implementation to ensure success. It becomes unique through its proven ability to strengthen ties between long-range plans and short-term allocation of funds as well as broad participation by external and internal stakeholders.

Three primary groups provide support to the strategic planning system. The CAC is the key leadership group aligning planning with resource allocation and deploying agreed-upon action plans. The Strategic Planning Committee has 16 members, including faculty, staff, and student representation and a strong membership connection to the CAC. The committee is responsible for developing and maintaining viable mission, vision, and values statements and long-term goals. It also develops strategic performance indicators and monitors the implementation of action plans. The last group is the Office of Budget, Planning, and Analysis (BPA), which has a staff of eight and includes the functions of institutional research, fiscal analyses, annual operating budget development, and capital budget development. This combination of functions has strengthened the use of data in informed decision-making, coordinates an inclusive planning process, aligns resources with strategies, provides objective data and information, and supports the process to measure university performance against indicators and targets.

Figure 2.2
The Strategic Planning Model at the University of Wisconsin—Stout

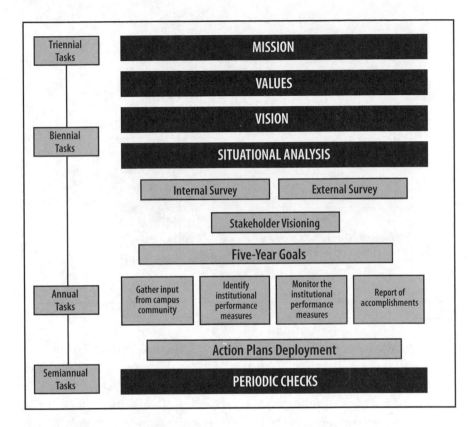

Annual Budget Priorities Process

The annual budget priorities process was the first significant change implemented at UW–Stout as part of the redesign of the strategic planning process. Early success in funding and deploying short-term priorities has led to the reallocation of funds or identification of new funding sources for over 45 priorities since 1996. The five-step process engages the campus in priority planning, allows multiple opportunities and methods for participation, and communicates final results to establish expectations and motivate performance (see Figure 2.3).

Figure 2.3

The Annual Budget Priorities Process at the University of Wisconsin–Stout

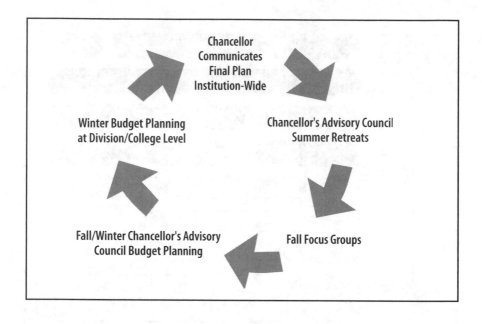

Step 1: CAC summer retreat. The process begins with the CAC preparing for the summer retreat. This is a four-month process that involves the review and discussion of information prepared by BPA. Typically, the information reviewed falls into the categories of emerging issues at the national, state, and local levels; current strategic plan and campus action plans; enrollment management; past and current priorities; university-wide performance data; survey data; and financial information. The CAC then holds a summer retreat to draft short-term planning priorities using a priority template. The retreats are facilitated and include warm-ups, small-group work, and large-group discussion. Various quality tools are used to facilitate discussion and prompt creative thinking.

Step 2: Fall facilitated sessions. In early fall, nine facilitated groups of faculty, staff, students, and CAC members discuss the draft short-term planning priorities. The focus group sessions encourage faculty, staff, and students to engage in direct, unfiltered, unedited communication with university administration on the draft of university priorities. More than 30% of university employees attend these sessions and provide feedback directly at the meeting. Other employees provide feedback through survey cards, via a university message board, or through their governance or organizational structure.

Step 3: Fall/winter CAC budget planning. Subsequently, two CAC budget planning sessions are held to review resource principles (see Figure 2.4) and input from the sessions, complete the strategies to implement short-term planning priorities, establish measures of performance, and recommend resource needs. A template has been developed to ensure that each priority is guided by these key questions:

- What issue is being solved?

- What solution is being proposed?

- How will the linkage to the strategic plan be demonstrated?

- What has to be done for this priority to succeed?

- Who are the positions or people that will be responsible for each step?

- What is the timeline?

- What resources are needed for this priority to succeed (human, physical, fiscal, other)?

- What information will be collected to benchmark and measure the priority's success?

Step 4: Winter budget planning at the division/college level. After the CAC makes recommendations on funding for short-term priorities, the chancellor will establish budget planning allocations at the division and major unit level. Throughout this process, complementary budget planning occurs at the division, college, and unit levels, and the specific budget detail is developed. While decentralized budget development is maintained, BPA provides training and support to budgeters as they develop individual account budgets. BPA ensures that budgets balance to targets at the college and major unit levels. These units provide summary information on budget decisions, reallocation decisions, and budget actions to support budget objectives.

Step 5: Chancellor communicates final plan institution wide. Once budget planning is finalized, the chancellor holds two university-wide budget forums to communicate final decisions on university priorities and resource allocations. The BPA office monitors progress on each priority action plan. All priority action plans are updated and shared with the CAC on a semiannual basis to ensure that sufficient progress is being made.

Figure 2.4
Resource Principles at the University of Wisconsin–Stout

Resource principles provide the framework for budget/resource allocation decisions. These principles recognize the variety of funding and resources and encourage creativity and flexibility in financing strategic plans. They also require awareness and integration of campus planning at all levels in order to effectively allocate budget and resources.

- Identify budget priorities through the use of participatory processes, guided by the mission statement and strategic planning.
- Fund activities that are central to the mission, add value, or are required.
- Protect the integrity of the undergraduate and graduate mission.
- Protect the integrity of services supporting the central university mission.
- Maintain flexibility at all levels of the organization through the use of reserves to fund strategic initiatives, emergencies, and other discretionary purposes.
- Reallocate resources to provide funding for high-priority strategic initiatives.
- Ensure near-term allocation decisions complement longer-term planning.
- Manage operations within allocated resources.
- Make informed budget decisions through the use of data, analyses, and projections.

Visioning

Situational analysis is an important part of visioning, and UW–Stout uses the SWOT (Strengths, Weaknesses, Opportunities, and Threats) methodology as the framework for its visioning process. The SWOT analysis allows the organization to identify its internal strengths and weaknesses, and provides an external survey of threats and opportunities. The Malcolm Baldrige National Quality Award feedback report clearly identifies overall institutional strengths and opportunities for improvement and is a valuable input to situational analysis.

Stakeholder visioning allows the organization to balance priorities between the future needs of the UW System and UW–Stout with its internal and external stakeholders. UW–Stout performed stakeholder visioning in 2001 and again in 2003. Quality tools are used to process stakeholder work sessions and result in succinct recommendations for future directions. Futurists and higher education experts often assist in the process. The most recent stakeholder visioning session utilized scenario planning to develop alternate approaches to an environment of fiscal uncertainty and expectation for transformation of education.

Performance Indicators

UW–Stout identifies performance indicators for the university's goals, priorities, and action plans. Levels of success are measured and performance is monitored by benchmarking and establishing targets or outcomes for each strategic goal and university priority. Performance indicators require solid data and information sources. This is a critical support role of BPA. Importantly, performance indicators align with UW–Stout's values, are reviewed annually, focus attention on areas needing improvement, and communicate expectations widely to faculty, staff, and students. Where UW–Stout's performance demonstrates clear leadership, the objective is to sustain that leadership. In other indicators, the objective is to close gaps to achieve greater competitive levels in all key performance measures.

Student and Stakeholder Focus

Identifying and satisfying the unique needs and expectations of student groups and other stakeholders is primary input for developing UW–Stout's strategies and achieving its mission. The mission of the UW System and UW–Stout determines which markets the educational programs will address. One of the primary goals of the UW System is to "provide widespread access to graduates of Wisconsin high schools." Therefore, the primary market for UW–Stout's programs is Wisconsin residents. The special mission of UW–Stout is to offer a select number of undergraduate and graduate programs in specialized fields not duplicated in the state or region. These specialized programs appeal to state residents (70% of students) and to students from 26 other states and 30 nations. The university accepts a limited number of nonresident students to meet enrollment and diversity goals.

UW System's market research unit assists UW–Stout in identifying markets for new programs. UW–Stout further segments these markets to target potential students who have characteristics that best fit UW–Stout's mission focus. This segmentation analysis is used primarily to develop programs targeted to serve and recruit high school students (such as the summer technology and engineering program), and students attending technical and community colleges who are interested in transferring (degree completion programs). Each year, the admissions office establishes application targets for each student segment.

Listening to and Learning From Students

UW–Stout student needs, expectations, and attitudes are assessed and monitored throughout the students' entire academic careers. During orientation, students are required to complete placement tests, a computer skills assessment, and fill out other special-needs surveys. The results are analyzed to determine appropriate course placement, identify special needs for housing and computer resources, and develop new student programming. Each student identifying a special need is contacted by a student services representative and referred to a support unit. Support units exist to meet the needs of new students, academically at-risk students, disabled students, minority students, transfer students, international students, and graduate students. Freshmen also participate in the National Survey of Student Engagement (NSSE) and a UW System survey of incoming student satisfaction.

Students are segmented by academic program and are actively involved in decision-making regarding their program. Program directors are key contacts for students and obtain information on student needs through formal advisement meetings and informal contact. Each program has an advisory committee composed of students, faculty, alumni and employers. Each semester, students evaluate courses, and academic programs are reviewed on a regular cycle to determine if they are meeting all stakeholder needs.

To proactively seek student needs and expectations, students participate in advisory committees for all major student service units including
the Library Learning Center, the Student Center, and the Multicultural
Services Advisory Council. Support units also obtain informal input from
students through suggestion boards, surveys, focus groups, and taste tests
(in dining services), and from the annual ACT Student Opinion Survey
administered to sophomores and juniors. Prior to graduation, students
complete an assessment of their general education competencies and the
NSSE Senior Survey. The results of these assessments are used to improve
students' future academic competencies and experiences.

BPA aggregates and analyzes longer-term needs and expectations from
demographic studies; student, alumni, and employer survey feedback;
information from environmental scans; and peer or best-practice comparisons. This office analyzes local, state, regional, and national data,
such as high school graduation projections and adult student markets, to
predict longer-term trends affecting enrollments, and participates in UW
System-wide strategic planning to anticipate and project changing student
requirements.

Knowledge of Stakeholder Needs and Expectations

UW–Stout has long-standing partnerships with its primary stakeholder
groups including alumni, employers, feeder schools, the community, UW
System, and the board of regents (see Figure 2.5). Alumni needs and
expectations are identified through the Stout Foundation contact processes and through alumni follow-up surveys. The Stout Foundation hosts
alumni gatherings throughout the world and maintains an alumni database and an interactive web site. In addition, the ACT Alumni Outcomes
Survey is used to provide nationally-normed alumni information.

The placement and co-op office develops and maintains strong relationships with area employers. Employers are listed on the UW–Stout
web site and in the online vacancy bulletin, and participate in a two-day
career conference each fall. The placement office coordinates on-campus
employer interviews. UW–Stout has more employers attend its career
conference than any other UW System comprehensive university. To
be proactive regarding employer needs, the placement and co-op office
installed software connecting students and employers with 24/7 online

Figure 2.5

Primary Stakeholder Groups and Key Success Measures at the University of Wisconsin–Stout

Stakeholder	Key Success Measures
Students	• Retention and graduation rates • Student satisfaction • Placement success in degree
Alumni	• Alumni satisfaction • Donations and contributions
Employers, business, and industry	• Placement rates • Employer satisfaction • New programs and services
Community and feeder schools	• Safety performance • Community service/involvement • Enrollment targets met • Transfers-in and graduation success
UW System and board of regents	• Accreditation performance • Budget and audit conformance • Board of regent member satisfaction

services. To evaluate the effectiveness of theses services, the placement office tracks graduates and BPA surveys employers.

UW–Stout also identifies the needs of its business and industry partners through three outreach units: the Stout Technology Park, the Stout Technology Transfer Institute (STTI), and the Stout Vocational Rehabilitation Institute (SVRI). The Stout Technology Park was established in 1990 and presently houses 48 manufacturing and service industries. Each tenant in the park has an ongoing relationship with UW–Stout and with faculty serving in consultant roles to the various organizations. Within STTI are several centers including the Northwest Wisconsin Manufacturing Outreach Center, which is funded by the National Institute of Standards and Technology. This award-winning center assists manufacturers in 33 counties to improve performance. SVRI is a large campus-based rehabilitation operation providing a wide array of resources and services to employers and to people with workplace disabilities.

As the largest employer in the city of Menomonie, UW–Stout senior leaders meet regularly with community leaders, and university faculty and staff serve on key community governance groups. The university and community also work together on major projects, such as the development of a new athletic/recreation complex on UW–Stout's campus. The UW System Board of Regents is a key stakeholder, and senior leaders meet with the board monthly to discuss issues. Expressed needs from these stakeholders are summarized during CAC monthly meetings and used in planning to develop future improvements.

Building Relationships With Students and Stakeholders

UW–Stout begins building relationships with students several years before they enroll. Middle and high school students are introduced to UW–Stout through precollege programs and campus preview days. Admissions counselors and program directors visit high schools and technical colleges to develop relationships with students and to foster positive referrals. In a nationwide high school guidance counselor survey done by *Newsweek/ Kaplan College Catalog* in 2001, UW–Stout was one of only four schools cited as a school most often recommended as a "hidden treasure," and a school that respondents would attend if they could repeat their college years.

Once students are enrolled, key student relationship objectives ensure student academic and social development, satisfaction with support services, and career placement. The primary method used to build and maintain relationships with students is interaction with program directors, faculty, and support staff. For students with special needs, or specific segments of students, relationships are also built and maintained through support services and peer organizations. BPA continually surveys all students throughout their academic career to monitor satisfaction with programs and services.

UW–Stout has formal complaint management processes for all stake-holders that are outlined in the *Wisconsin Administrative Code*. Processes are also described in the handbooks provided to employees and students. UW–Stout's complaint policy is to address each complaint at the source but provide for an escalation path when required. In offices that receive formal complaints, the complaints and their resolutions are documented and aggregated campus wide. A formal review of complaint trends is conducted by the CAC twice each year with action plans formed to address issues.

Sources of current information on student and stakeholder needs include survey feedback from students, alumni, and employers; input from advisory committees, campus councils, industry associations, and consultants; and participation in UW System research studies that are national in scope. These sources also provide a mechanism by which to compare UW–Stout listening and learning processes for efficiency and effectiveness to best practices.

Since 2001, UW–Stout faculty and senior leaders have been actively involved in the Academic Quality Improvement Program, the Quest for Excellence Conference, the National Consortium for Continuous Improvement in Higher Education, the Continuous Quality Improvement Network, and in sharing best practices with Baldrige Award recipients and with other educational institutions. Evaluations from state and national accrediting agencies also influence educational improvements.

Measurement, Information, and Analysis

UW–Stout's mission, values, and strategies provide the platform for selecting, analyzing, evaluating, and managing data and information to support student and stakeholder needs. This information is used to plan strategies and budgets, review and compare process performance, set goals, anticipate changing conditions, and to identify root causes and opportunities.

Performance Measurement and Analysis

By applying its mission, values, and stakeholder needs as a foundation for developing strategic goals and annual plans, UW–Stout has developed a four-step process to select, align, use, and improve its organizational performance measurement system. These steps include: 1) select key indicators that align to and provide an assessment of both strategic and annual progress; 2) identify goals based on comparisons and best practices; 3) ensure data integrity; and 4) evaluate the effectiveness of indicators in identifying cause and effect (see Figure 2.6).

UW–Stout's approach to data gathering is to enter data one time, in one place. To achieve this, the campus uses the concept of data ownership. Data and information requirements identified as part of the strategic planning process are organized into three primary operational areas: 1) academic and student data are gathered from the four schools and col-

Figure 2.6
The Performance Measurement System at the University of Wisconsin–Stout

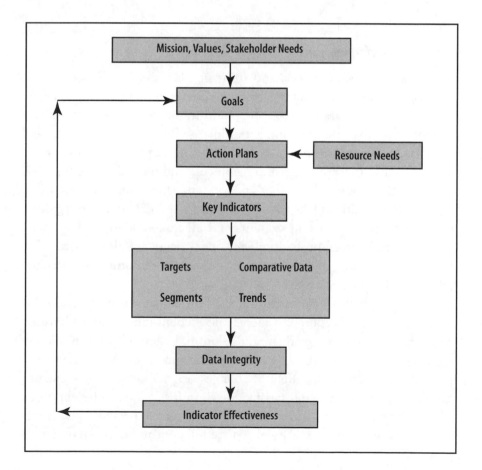

leges and consolidated in the academic and student affairs division, 2) business, human resource, and safety data are gathered from student and support service areas and integrated in the administrative and student life services division, and 3) information technology operational information is collected and integrated by the chief information officer. Further, BPA collects and integrates operational results to determine short-term performance and results of studies and surveys for use in longer-term planning.

UW–Stout uses an integrated relational database (Datatel) to consolidate and retrieve university-wide information. Critical information integrated at the divisional level is further incorporated for organization-wide, short-term decision-making at the CAC and actions deployed through the various councils, committees, and governance organizations. Longer-term analysis is integrated during the strategic reviews and CAC summer retreats.

Developing Performance Indicators

UW–Stout's mission, values, and strategic plan are the criteria used to develop the most important organizational measures and goals (see Figure 2.7). UW–Stout uses the strategic planning process to develop strategic goals, annual priorities, and action plans. Performance measures and indicators to monitor operational and long-term progress toward goals are selected in the strategic planning process and refined by the Strategic Planning Committee. UW–Stout's performance indicators are designed to address the breadth and depth of its operations, including tracking groups; create a balanced focus on students and all stakeholders; and evaluate university-wide processes performance. These data are also structured to facilitate root cause determination by segmenting information into specific groups and categories.

For example, UW–Stout can track the total academic life-cycle performance and satisfaction of students and student groups from admission to graduation and after graduation as alumni. Unlimited segmentation of student data (for example, by academic program or gender) provides the flexibility to analyze the effect of changes on unique student segments. Similarly, performance and satisfaction data for each stakeholder group (for example, employer satisfaction with graduates' specific skills) is segmented, providing the capacity to analyze relationships between outcomes and processes.

Figure 2.7
Key Performance Indicators at the University of Wisconsin–Stout

Student Performance Results • Student learning • ACT composite scores • New freshman retention • Supplemental instruction • Program competencies • Active learning • Student competencies developed • Student appreciation of diversity • Graduation rate • Placement success • Overall program effectiveness **Faculty and Staff Results** • Faculty and staff morale • Leadership evaluation • Employee satisfaction • Faculty turnover • Classified staff grievances • Faculty diversity • Highest educational level • Professional develoment expenditures • Professorships and chairs • Human resources effectiveness • Injury/accident rate	**Student and Stakeholder Satisfaction** • Freshman evaluation • Student satisfaction • Alumni satisfaction with instruction • Employer satisfaction with graduates • Board of regents satisfaction • Recognition **Budgetary and Financial Results** • Affordable tuition, room, board • Revenue growth • Budget priority funding • Support for instruction • Budget flexibility **Organizational Effectiveness** • Distinctive array of programs • Curriculum renewal • Extramural funding • Lab-based instruction • FTE enrollment • Distance learning delivery • Audit compliance • Safety and security • Support service performance • Information technology performance • Satisfaction with support services

Use of Comparative Data

UW–Stout selects comparative data based on the following criteria:

- Best appropriate noneducational or educational organization comparisons establish national leadership goals and performance levels for strategic indicators

- UW System, mission-similar universities (Ferris State College, California Polytechnic State University, and New Jersey Institute of Technology), and other nationally known higher education institutions establish national higher education best practices and stretch goals for process improvement

- UW System and UW comprehensive comparisons and best practices establish leadership in the primary market

In addition, comparative data needs are routinely identified as part of the regular program and unit review processes requiring comparisons with peer and competitor institutions and against national, state, and peer best practices. UW–Stout process improvement actions and/or performance review results also highlight comparative information needs, and accreditation reviews require program-focused comparative data.

UW System comparative data complement and extend its own processes for obtaining comparative and benchmark data. UW–Stout employs national standards and reports such as the Common Data Set and National Center for Education Statistics data, Integrated Postsecondary Education Data System data, and information developed by national organizations such as the College and University Personnel Association, and the National Association of College and University Business Officers. The university participates in national, normative surveys such as the ACT Student Opinion Survey. Benchmarking efforts for public institutions sponsored by the American Association of State Colleges and Universities, Educational Benchmarking, Inc., and the Consortium for Student Retention Data Exchange; graduation and retention studies; and the American Productivity and Quality Center's budgeting study are utilized.

Performance Analysis

UW–Stout's data-driven decision-making uses a full range of analytic tools to plan and evaluate university performance. At a macro level, the board of regents, governor, legislature, and key state agencies develop plans, incentives, disincentives, and mandates to be analyzed for strategic impact. UW–Stout senior leaders participate in structured summits and task forces to discuss educational issues with national leaders brought to the state by the UW System.

The CAC summer retreats are the primary mechanism for addressing overall organizational health and strategic planning. All units prepare projections encompassing all areas of the university to be used in planning. For example, managers of auxiliary units project five-year business plans addressing expected fee rate changes, revenue, expenditures, reserve levels, capital plans, and debt service. Budget decisions, such as allocating additional funds to a particular service (e.g., fleet vehicles), rely on scenarios addressing solvency projections and comparative pricing/availability data. Inferential statistics, such as correlations, factor analysis, and regression, are used to analyze surveys and in database-grounded studies of such issues as salary equity and faculty workload.

Information Management

UW–Stout employs a user-centric approach to information management. The underlying principle is availability of the right data, to the right constituency, by their preferred method, at the right time. UW–Stout's approach is to put as much of its essential information on the web site as possible. Students, faculty, and staff access data and information on UW–Stout's high-speed, fully redundant computer network and through web access in all administrative buildings, classrooms, and residence hall rooms. Constituents communicate via email, and the network provides rapid access to all essential data housed in Datatel. UW–Stout's *Factbook*, an extensive set of trends and comparative information on students, faculty, and programs, is kept current on the web site.

A campus portal has been developed so students can register, access financial aid data, account information, and grades, and maintain their resumes on the web site. Faculty members readily access student data and all institutional research reports via the web site. Performance reports can be easily customized on any database dimension. When new applications are introduced, training is provided to the appropriate user community. As evidence of their commitment to information access and use, UW–Stout was the first university in the UW System to make laptops mandatory for all incoming freshmen. Faculty and staff computers, which are primarily laptops, are replaced every three years. Further, UW–Stout is also the leader in UW System data warehousing.

UW–Stout employs a broad approach to ensure high-quality data, system, and network integrity. This approach encompasses concepts that are critical in providing the information necessary for accurate, effective, and timely access. The university's chief information officer and the technology and information services department are responsible for evaluating, maintaining, and improving the university's information infrastructure.

Faculty and Staff Focus

At UW–Stout, the human resources system model is designed to support the university's mission, vision, values, and strategic plan (see Figure 2.8). The model encompasses organization, career, and succession planning, selection and retention of employees, and performance management. UW–Stout's organization encompasses a traditional academic departmental structure, with student service units and administrative support units. Each position has a clearly defined job description, and each work unit has established goals and objectives.

To make this traditional structure effective in achieving student development needs and a high degree of cooperation and flexibility, UW–Stout's work system integrates the faculty and staff in departments through a collaborative set of established committees and other cross-functional structures. Shared governance, consisting of the three senates, represents the highest-level cross-functional work system entity. Within each of the senates are numerous established committees with broad, campus-wide participation. The senates and committees provide a structured process for each individual within the organization to bring forth new ideas that can be addressed at the senate level or taken to the CAC for university-wide consideration.

The majority of the classified staff members are represented by one of five state unions. UW–Stout has a cooperative and collaborative relationship with all of these unions. Human resources holds monthly union/

Figure 2.8

The Human Resource System at the University of Wisconsin–Stout

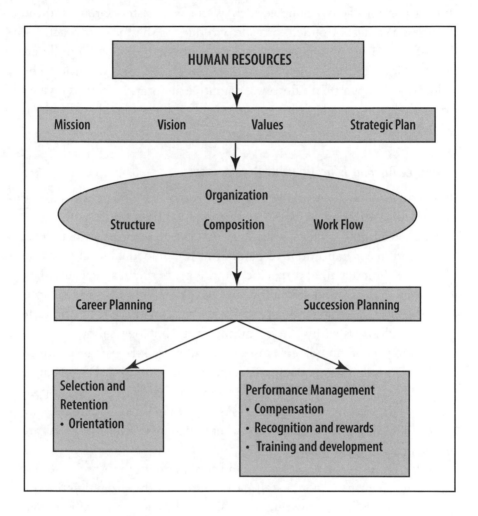

management meetings with the objective of identifying and preventing potential problems before they lead to grievances. A Classified Advisory Council was formed to develop a recognition award for classified staff, to recommend a comprehensive classified development program, and to serve as a sounding board for campus issues.

Best practices are shared across campus through user groups, peer councils, colloquiums, celebrations, and training programs. Examples of sharing effective teaching practices include college teaching seminars, a lessons learned series, and web camps. Groups with members who hold similar positions across campus, such as the Webmasters Group and the Business Managers Council, provide a venue for sharing best practices. UW–Stout's work-system structures are continually evaluated to determine their effectiveness in achieving short- and long-term strategies. The Educational Support Unit Review Committee performs scheduled reviews of all student service and support units and provides formal feedback on effectiveness.

Employee Training, Education, and Development

Education, training, and career and professional development needs are identified at three levels: 1) at the campus-wide level for developmental needs linked to the strategic direction, 2) at the division/department level to support major unit initiatives, and 3) at the individual level to satisfy discipline, functional, and specific requirements such as licensure. Key organizational education, training, and developmental needs are identified as part of the strategic planning process to support the seven strategic goals. At all levels within the organization, technology, safety, continuous improvement, and diversity issues are addressed. For areas identified in the planning process, targeted programs are developed. For example, diversity was developed as a focused process with goals, strategies, responsibilities, and benchmarks identified. As key needs are identified, they are assigned to an organizational office where ongoing training programs are developed and supported.

UW–Stout uses both informal and formal orientation processes for new hires. New faculty and staff participate in a three-day orientation program each fall covering campus mission and values, organization, policies, health and benefits, parking and security, and electronic mail. A series of college teaching seminars is held each fall for new faculty and instructional staff and includes topics such as analyzing student characteristics, course design, cooperative learning methods, and student assessment. Faculty and staff are also initiated into the culture and traditions of the campus through convocations, all-college meetings, new employee receptions, and a mentoring program.

UW–Stout uses a variety of methods to deliver its education and training, including web-based training, consultants, professional trainers, and UW–Stout faculty and staff who deliver on-campus workshops. These workshops are open to all employees. In addition, the university sends hundreds of faculty and staff off campus to training workshops, conferences, and seminars sponsored by the UW System, professional associations, or private companies. A yearlong leadership and professional development program for midlevel managers is offered by the campus each year and addresses the following areas: self-management, change, working together effectively, communication and personal effectiveness, managing conflict, customer-centered programs, decision-making and problem solving, and frontline leadership.

Internal training is evaluated for participant satisfaction. Some areas require knowledge or skill testing. The primary method to determine overall training effectiveness is through survey feedback and monitoring operational performance improvement in areas where training has been targeted, such as safety, information technology, and diversity. Knowledge and skills are reinforced on the job through observation, application of skills, and monitoring performance indicators. For example, department chairs observe and evaluate classroom instructors. Supervisors require employees to produce work using new software programs. Monitoring the Computer Center help desk calls provides important information on the effectiveness of information technology training delivered. Knowledge gained is shared through reports at staff meetings, brown-bag lunches, or through articles in newsletters.

UW–Stout's strategic objectives require that faculty and staff develop new skills that complement and extend their learning and student development capabilities. For example, when the university identified information technology skills as necessary for all employees and students, monthly training programs were provided for standardized software applications, and a computer cost-share program was developed to encourage departments to acquire and maintain current technology for all employees. Web camps were initiated for faculty and staff. A lab renewal plan was developed to ensure students and faculty would have access to current instructional technology, and classrooms were updated to provide a mediated environment.

Performance Evaluation

Probationary faculty, academic staff, and classified staff are reviewed annually as part of the performance evaluation process. Post-tenure review for faculty occurs every five years. As part of the faculty and academic staff evaluation, a merit code is assigned and used to determine employee compensation. For tenured faculty, the performance evaluation process is used to set five-year mutually agreed-upon goals with supporting training and professional development plans. The post-tenure review process provides the opportunity for individuals to assess their accomplishments over an extended period of time and to set future goals. Student evaluations of teachers' classroom performance are also used for performance evaluation and improvement. UW–Stout is consistently among the leaders in the UW System comprehensive universities in professional development expenditures, sabbaticals, and professorships.

UW–Stout's performance review process for faculty and academic staff includes an affirmative action/equal employment opportunity assessment for all supervisors. The classified performance review includes an assessment for supervisors covering actions and activities in support of the university's diversity plan. Compensation and recognition practices are designed to reward high performance, be equitable, and recognize longevity and loyalty to the institution. There is strong governance involvement in establishing compensation systems within UW Board of Regents guidelines and with chancellor approval. The compensation systems provide merit awards, adjustments for promotion and educational preparation changes, and address longevity and salary equity issues.

Faculty and Staff Well-Being and Satisfaction

Survey feedback, benchmarking, grievances, exit interviews, monitoring absenteeism and turnover, and other informal listening posts, such as attendance at campus gatherings and participation in governance, are used to gather information on the key factors affecting employee well-being, satisfaction, and motivation. Key factors include professional work life, reward systems, evaluation systems, collegial and job relations, governance and classified representation, personal factors, leadership, and the overall work environment. Indicators are reviewed annually during the planning process to highlight trends in order to prioritize actions to address performance gaps, issues, or opportunities, and to determine how well UW–Stout is achieving its goals.

Benchmarking studies, surveys, focus groups, and reports provide segmented data by various groups (gender, race, and classification of employment) in order to understand the needs and opportunities of different groups of employees. For example, an Equality for Women Committee was formed to examine the issues surrounding the female segment of the workforce.

Comprehensive morale surveys of employees are conducted every three years with a one-minute climate survey conducted in the alternate years. A committee developed UW–Stout's comprehensive morale survey by benchmarking a number of higher education morale surveys and then recommending a model published by the College and University Personnel Association. Statistical analysis of survey results evaluates employee group, organization, key factors, and campus-wide issues, highlighting differences among groups. Key issues and opportunities are identified as part of the annual CAC summer retreat—the first step in the process to identify short-term university priorities. As appropriate, action plans are identified, university priorities are drafted, and the workplace organization is considered to address concerns.

Process Management

UW–Stout's educational programs and support processes are designed and deployed to achieve its value of "excellence in teaching within high quality, student-centered education involving active learning and appropriate technology."

Design and Delivery of Educational Processes

UW–Stout offers a focused set of 27 undergraduate and 17 graduate degree programs that are closely aligned to its mission. As stakeholder demand or new opportunities surface through the planning process, UW–Stout will develop and implement new degree programs. In the new program development process, the university uses several sources of data to evaluate needs and expectations for new programs: current and projected job market trends, information on employer needs, student and alumni demographics, competition, and current and future student interests. Based on this input, faculty, staff, and administrators develop ideas for new programs to be included in the campus academic plan, which is updated quarterly by the Provost's Council.

For new degree programs, the faculty, in consultation with employers and other stakeholders, develops a preliminary proposal and routes the proposal through the campus approval process. Criteria used in the review process include program consistency with the university mission, evidence of employers' need for the program, potential student audience, intended student outcomes, impact on existing program offerings, and resource requirements. Once degree proposals are approved on campus, they are sent to the UW System for approval.

Upon approval, a program director is appointed and a program advisory committee, including representatives from professionals in the field, is formed. After the program advisory committee is in place, a formal needs assessment is conducted to determine the skills and competencies to be included in the curriculum. The program advisory committee then develops a seven-part comprehensive implementation plan: 1) program goals and objectives, 2) curriculum, 3) faculty and staff expertise, 4) recruiting strategies, 5) enrollment projections, 6) assessment strategies, and 7) resource information (see Figure 2.9).

New degree programs often include a combination of new and existing courses. Each course specifies required entry competencies, performance objectives, learning activities, and evaluation criteria. The implementation plan and accompanying curriculum must be reviewed by two external consultants, by the UW System, and by the board of regents.

As part of the campus strategy, more programs are being designed and modified to provide greater flexibility and access to accommodate differing student and stakeholder needs through new technological delivery systems. For example, to meet the needs of hospitality professionals located worldwide, the university redesigned the hospitality and tourism program graduate degree to be delivered completely online. An undergraduate degree in industrial management is offered via a combination of technologies throughout the state to its target audience of place-bound adults with full-time jobs.

Figure 2.9
The Program Development Process at the University of Wisconsin–Stout

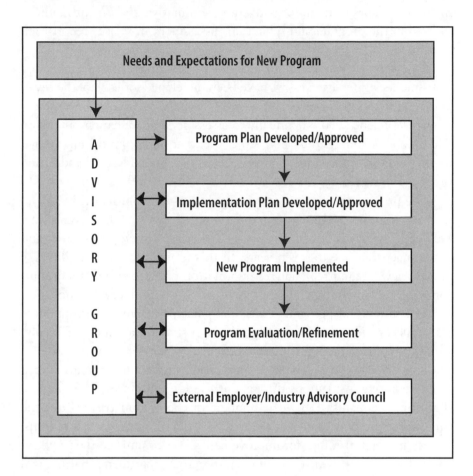

Assessment of Student Learning and Academic Programs

Each program director develops an assessment plan containing formative and summative assessment techniques to determine if the program is achieving its intended learning outcomes. Formative assessment occurs as the students progress through the program, which involves evaluation of course assignments and examinations, mid-program reviews, or admission into "advanced standing" in a program. Summative assessment methods vary by program and may include certification exams, evaluations from internship supervisors or student teacher supervisors, student portfolios, or performance in capstone courses. Each program director must document the results from all formative and summative assessment methods utilized in the program and submit an "assessment in major" report each year.

Assessment tools in the form of objective exams, course-embedded assessments, and written essays have been developed for each of the seven general education categories. The ACT Collegiate Assessment of Academic Proficiency is used annually to assess general education outcomes. The campus evaluates the value of the e-scholar (laptop) program through a series of faculty and student surveys, focus groups, analysis of grades, and other performance indicators.

The program review process is utilized to systematically review all degree programs and identify improvement opportunities. The timing between reviews is dependent on the findings of previous reviews and may range from one to seven years. In this formal process, the Planning and Review Committee analyzes information on enrollment trends, currency of course content, instructional methods, delivery technologies, assessment methods, program costs, and placement rates. The committee also collects additional information through student, alumni, and faculty surveys, and from program advisory committee members.

This information is compared with data from similar programs offered at comparative institutions throughout the United States. The program director, in consultation with members of the committee, utilizes the information to develop a self-study report detailing program strengths, issues, and opportunities for improvement. The committee then reviews the self-study report with the program director, department chair(s), and the dean and prepares a summary report. The dean develops a response to the report detailing action plans to address recommendations. In some cases, a short-term action plan and a status report documenting improvements after a one-year period are required.

Educational Support Processes

Educational Support Services are designed and delivered to enhance UW–Stout academic programs and to facilitate active learning, student success, and student and stakeholder satisfaction. Support service needs are determined through two primary methods: 1) top-down identification of needs from strategy development or the planning process, and 2) from surveys and other student and stakeholder feedback. Each year, students are asked to identify needs and determine budget priorities as part of the campus-wide budget planning process. Students are also surveyed annually on all student services using the ACT Student Opinion Survey. External feedback on services is gained through alumni gatherings and employer surveys. External regulations may also require changes in facilities or services. When new needs are identified, the CAC determines budget requirements for support services and works out budget priorities with the campus organizations. Input received from student surveys and stakeholder feedback has resulted in budgeting additional dollars and providing additional resources in the areas of library access, laboratory availability, and co-op and placement services.

Most student services are not new, but to meet the changing needs of students, many of these traditional processes are being continually expanded and/or redesigned using the continuous improvement process. Support process owners, typically unit directors, are responsible for evaluating and improving their processes. They use surveys and other feedback to evaluate service quality. They benchmark other service providers using data from other academic institutions, internal analysis, and applying data from the private sector when appropriate. From this analysis, improvements are recommended, budgeted, and implemented.

These changes are monitored to assess effectiveness of improvements in satisfying the original student, stakeholder, or university objectives. For example, in response to student and stakeholder feedback, open hours in many student service areas have been extended to evenings or weekends, and other services have been made available online. Student satisfaction with support services is essential as many of these areas are funded primarily by user fees. In addition to formal benchmark surveys, the support service units utilize a number of operational feedback and control mechanisms to obtain student input. Student satisfaction with student services is measured and compared to other universities annually through the ACT Student Opinion Survey.

Further, the Educational Support Unit Review Committee (see Figure 2.10) performs annual reviews of support service units on a rotational basis. As part of this process, student, faculty, staff, and other stakeholder input is collected, and campuses are compared to the UW–Stout unit being reviewed on each service area. In addition to the ACT survey and the Educational Support Unit Review process, all student service units utilize the specific data to review and improve operations on a continuing basis. The result of this continuous improvement process is a campus environment that provides high-quality support services. Survey results indicate that UW–Stout students are more satisfied than students at other campuses in areas such as library services, financial aid, and the student center.

Figure 2.10
Educational Support Unit Review at the University of Wisconsin–Stout

Objectives: Continuously examine and improve services and management processes in response to changing university needs.

- Examine units in relation to the following criteria: centrality to mission, demand or need for services, quality, cost effectiveness, and comparative advantage.

- Identify management, organizational and budget flexibilities, both long and short term, to address university budget priorities.

- Increase communication, knowledge, and understanding among university departments, units, and services.

- Review units and functions using both quantitative—including benchmarking—and qualitative measures, fully engaging the units being reviewed in the study.

3

Monfort College of Business, University of Northern Colorado

Gerald L. Shadwick

The Kenneth W. Monfort College of Business is one of five academic colleges within the University of Northern Colorado, a publicly supported institution serving 11,000 students. The College of Business was established in 1968 as an autonomous, degree-recommending unit, and through the 1970s paralleled a national trend for business schools of explosive enrollment growth. By 1984, the college was serving over 2,000 students enrolled in one of several undergraduate, master's, and doctoral degree programs. Although the college was producing large quantities of graduates, it was agreed that overall program quality could be improved by focusing resources on a narrower range of degree options. In the mid-1980s, the mission was revised to "high-quality, undergraduate-only business education." All graduate programs were phased out, and the number of undergraduate degree programs was narrowed to one, a bachelor of science in business administration.

In 1992, the college reached its goal of accreditation by the Association to Advance Collegiate Schools of Business. In 1999, with a $10.5 million commitment from the Monfort Family Foundation, the name was officially changed to the Kenneth W. Monfort College of Business. Also in 1999, the college was recognized by the Colorado Commission on Higher

Education as a Program of Excellence. The college has been utilizing the Baldrige education criteria since 2000.

Leadership System

The college's mission, vision, and values articulate the basic principles for its continuous improvement activities. The leadership system is built around a framework of systematic decision-making, collaboration from within and outside the organization, and a uniform commitment to mission. The senior leaders of the Monfort College of Business (MCB) include the dean (who reports to the university's provost), an associate and assistant dean, and the Administrative Council. The senior leaders, utilizing the process of shared governance, revise, set, and deploy the values and the short- and long-term direction for the college and establish performance expectations in accordance with the vision and mission of the college. Embedded in the process of building business excellence are commitments by the college's senior leaders to create value for students, to build a high-quality business education program, and to be unique by comparison to its competition. These commitments include the following:

- All college resources are devoted to delivering a high-quality, focused, undergraduate-only business program

- Provide value to students by offering quality education at a competitive price

- Well-designed curriculum policies and physical facilities that limit class sizes and promote interaction between faculty, students, and the business community

- An assurance that the faculty will be academically qualified with terminal degrees or professionally qualified with current business experience at the senior level

- A unique focus on the use of nationally known business executives who teach as resident faculty to complement the academic education provided by the full-time faculty

- Deployed technologies that extend well beyond the traditional computer labs of peer institutions and offer students industry-patterned facilities in which to learn

These commitments are maintained within a framework of MCB's program strategy of high-touch, wide-tech, and professional depth. This framework is shared with faculty and staff through numerous channels including meetings, newsletters, electronic communications, and SEDONA, a web-enabled database for business colleges.

The four standing faculty committees are an important part of the communication between the faculty and the college leadership team. These committees have specific, functionally driven charges and the power to make decisions on behalf of the faculty-at-large in areas of curriculum, student affairs, faculty affairs, and technology. Another major avenue through which top leaders obtain feedback from faculty is the Educational Benchmarking, Inc. (EBI) Faculty Satisfaction Survey. The college requests annual participation in this assessment activity from all full-time faculty. The instrument is anonymous, and results are shared with senior leaders and faculty through the governance structure.

The Administrative Council functions as a communications conduit between faculty members and the dean, and between academic chairs within the Administrative Council. Department chairs hold faculty meetings and individual conferences with faculty members to share topics discussed at council meetings and request feedback to be funneled back to the council. Formal communication with students is accomplished through mass communication vehicles (e.g., web site, mailings, email) and through the Student Representative Council and other student organizations. The college also utilizes a system of postings on classroom bulletin boards, announcements in classes, an open-door policy, and an innovative, electronic interface system housed on all student lab and classroom computers.

Legal and Ethical Behavior

The college and the university support an environment that expects legal and ethical behavior on the part of students and faculty. The university has worked with students to create a student honor code, and the university's student handbook clearly outlines ethical and legal behaviors. Each course syllabus includes an ethics statement, and ethics concepts are incorporated into each college course offering. In 2003, to proactively address ethics problems in business, a new course in fraud examination was initiated.

Faculty and staff are given training on ethical issues, and there are ethical standards for faculty activities. Management accountability for the organization's actions is an important evaluation component within the accreditation program of the Association to Advance Collegiate Schools of Business (AACSB). This international accrediting body periodically audits the college for evidence of performance measured against published standards. AACSB embraces a philosophy of continuous improvement, and accredited schools must employ periodic realignment of their programs and policies to ensure compliance with the standards.

Organizational Performance Review

Senior leaders use key performance indicators (KPIs) to gauge capacities and performance results. For example, each semester the Administrative Council reviews the utilization of instructional resources, student registrations, and admissions and establishes enrollment targets that match MCB's resources. This review includes comparing course enrollments to capacities to determine a precise number of class offerings to meet discipline emphasis standards and student demand. Targets are based on maintaining an average class size that is consistent with the college's instructional values.

Two primary tools used to evaluate and improve organizational performance are the EBI surveys and the Educational Testing Service (ETS) Major Field Exam. These instruments are recognized as the national standards for benchmarking by undergraduate business programs. The EBI instruments provide benchmarks on MCB faculty, student, and alumni experiences against comparable universities across the United States. Additionally, the EBI Benchmarking Study offers data on such areas as costs and student retention. College leadership and faculty committees develop specific target points for each specified KPI. Using these measures, the committees begin their processes of reviewing data based on set objectives.

KPIs are regularly reviewed by faculty committees, the Administrative Council, and the dean. Seniors and alumni also complete satisfaction surveys that provide important trend information that is then used in making adjustments to the educational program. Other statistical information, including reports on enrollment, diversity, and budget issues, is provided by university administration. The college shares performance review findings with the Administrative Council and the faculty committees. Each group is charged with reviewing results and developing program changes that will improve overall performance. For example, reviewing the results of the ETS Major Field Exam is a responsibility of the Curriculum Committee. Recent exam results indicated that performance on the economics portion of the exam was below target. This led the Committee to work with the economics department to improve coverage in that content area.

Through the SEDONA database system and published reports, all faculty members have access to information needed for suggesting improvements to senior leaders. Academic departments also use this data to evaluate and select courses of action for improvement. The dean shares findings from these reviews with key groups such as the Dean's Leadership Council to solicit external suggestions for helping to improve college programs.

Social Responsibility and Support of Key Communities

The college considers the Rocky Mountain Region and its people, businesses, and communities as its primary key community and uses a variety of measures to determine how its programs, offerings, services, and operations affect its community and society in general. In 2002, the dean reformed the former advisory board into a Dean's Leadership Council with an expanded role. Comprising 25 Colorado professionals and senior business leaders, the role of the Leadership Council is to provide a forum for interaction between the business community and the college. The college also has separate advisory boards of external leaders that work with the accounting department, the entrepreneurship program, and the nonprofit program. These boards are also responsible for providing direction, setting goals and expectations, and helping to keep the curriculum current and relevant in the respective areas.

In an effort to recognize its social responsibilities, the college has initiated a series of activities to provide learning opportunities for students and service to stakeholders. In cooperation with the University Foundation, a program called Business Plus brings leading national figures to campus for presentations to which the general public is invited. Two important service programs are the Summer Leadership Institute for Nonprofit Executives and the Youth Entrepreneurship Conference for students in grades 3 through 12.

MCB is an active supporter of important community programs such as the United Way. Faculty, senior leaders, staff members, and students are actively involved with these organizations through personal donations of their time and money. A number of classes include projects that directly impact the local community. The Small Business Institute is one such example of a class that has students working directly with local area businesses to provide college-supervised consulting services, while offering real-world business experience for students. Accounting students provide volunteer income tax assistance to the public through the Volunteer Income Tax Association Program, and a number of business students participate regularly in schools through the local Junior Achievement Chapter.

The college's nonprofit program subsidizes workshops for nonprofit executive directors to help them learn business principles and improve the effectiveness of their agencies. The program also prepares students for future employment in nonprofit organizations. The local mayor called upon the college to identify a qualified student team that could develop a business plan for the local community events center. A team of students was recruited within one week and completed a plan for this center.

Strategic Planning

The college's current strategic planning process has grown out of a university-wide planning process developed in 1994. The process includes a defined mission, an internal and external environmental analysis, and a set of KPIs. Also articulated were strategies for assuring quality, managing enrollments, and maintaining program relevancy over time. Over the next several years, the dean and members of the Administrative Council monitored key performance areas, set goals, and measured results on an annual basis.

In 2002, the college began a formal revision of its strategic plan and overall planning process that led to a revised mission, vision, and values document along with an updated set of KPIs. The revised process also includes a broader base of informational inputs from a number of key publics.

Strategy Development

Figure 3.1 illustrates the current strategic planning process that grew out of a series of planning sessions involving all MCB faculty and staff in 2001. This group completed a full review of the mission, vision, values, and objectives, and their recommendations were forwarded to the Administrative Council, which then developed a strategic planning format. The college utilizes information from internal and external sources, including a set of performance indicators, to form the basis for plan development. MCB has developed a set of KPIs, each of which threads back to a critical area within the college's processes. From this data, a series of short- and long-term goals are identified. These goals are reviewed annually in June. This review helps form the basis upon which the college realigns its priorities for plan implementation.

Strategies are deployed through the MCB governance structure, including the department chairs and college committees, with formal implementation beginning in September. An important part of MCB's strategic planning process is the development of expectations for strategy implementation. Goal accomplishment and time horizons are subject to adjustments, to reflect changes in personnel and budgets, and other changes in decision inputs.

The Administrative Council and other MCB committees monitor key performance data in cycle as it becomes available. The KPIs are then adjusted as needed to align with the strategic objectives. In 2003, for example, two state budget cuts required the college to make midyear adjustments in spending plans and in planning priorities.

Figure 3.1

The Strategic Planning Process at the Monfort College of Business

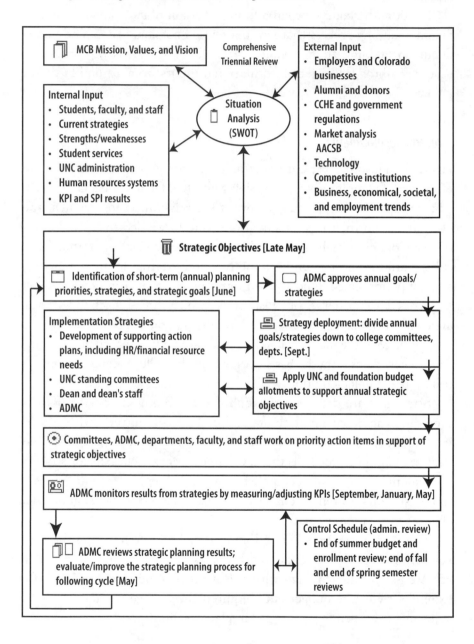

Strategic Objectives

The college's key strategic objectives reflect the organization's goals and challenges: 1) build a high-quality student population, 2) maintain a high-quality faculty, 3) maintain adequate financial resources, and 4) build a reputation in the marketplace that is consistent with program excellence (see Figure 3.2). These objectives are long term in nature and represent significant challenges. However, within the college's strategic plan, these key objectives serve as categories for a wide variety of short-term goals within the KPI control structure. The timetable for achieving these operational goals is set on a one- and five-year basis. Performance data are tracked through KPIs within the strategic planning document updated each June.

The strategic challenges of building a high-quality student population and maintaining a high-quality faculty are an ongoing responsibility. The challenge of maintaining adequate financial resources previously translated to being an efficient steward of state resources. The new reality involves dealing with severe cuts in funding, stemming from the passage of two Colorado constitutional amendments: the TABOR amendment, which significantly reduced state funding in tight economic times, and Amendment 23, which requires substantial increases in funding for K–12 education, thereby reducing the pool of money available for higher education. This has increased the need to raise private funds to ensure MCB continues as a high-quality undergraduate business program.

The challenge of building a positive reputation and stronger identity for MCB is a recent challenge embraced by the Administrative Council following the decision to revise the vision. A strong reputation for excellence is extremely important in attracting quality students, faculty, private funding, and employer stakeholders. To meet this challenge a number of actions have been implemented. An experienced public relations professional was recruited and hired as an executive professor in 2003 and charged with the redesign and expansion of MCB's marketing and public relations efforts. While too early to assign cause and effect, in 2004, freshman applications increased 30% from the previous year.

Figure 3.2

The Strategy Deployment Process at the Monfort College of Business

Strategic Objectives	Action Plans	KPI Tracking Measures
Build high-quality student population	• Finley scholarships • Improved high school contacts • MCB Listens program • Align curriculum to trends	• High-quality entering freshmen • Student satisfaction and retention rates • Student learning in business
Maintain high-quality faculty	• Nine-hour load standards • Faculty development • Professional development merit allocations	• Faculty academic qualification • Faculty program satisfaction • Faculty satisfaction
Maintain adequate financial resources	• Realign balance between tenured/nontenured faculty • Improve alumni support	• Total available state funds annually • Total available private funds annually
Develop market reputation consistent with program excellence	• Target low areas on EBI • Internship program • Improve alumni contacts • Improve employer contacts • External relations position	• Exiting student satisfaction • Placement of graduates • Alumni satisfaction • Employer satisfaction • Employer and alumni satisfaction, MCB media coverage

Strategy Deployment

The tactical action plans for achieving goals are formulated by the Administrative Council and the various faculty governance committees. This follows a thorough evaluation of the conditions, resources, and needs within the college. Each of the goals is derived from an examination of the college's KPIs and represents specific target areas that define the achievement of MCB's strategic objectives. Each KPI is a single issue action area (e.g., recruiting high-quality freshmen). This is followed by a current performance measure (e.g., entering freshmen ACT of 23.5 for fall 2003), which is then paired against a comparator measure (e.g., entering freshmen ACT of 23.3 for fall 2002). Following this information, goals are specified (one- and five-year targets). These goals have been derived through a discussion between the Administrative Council and dean that include comparisons to best-in-class performance levels when such information is available and appropriate.

Following the goal specifications is a listing of action plans (tactics) which the Administrative Council and relevant faculty committees determine to be appropriate in helping the college reach its designated goal targets. All of the KPI goal sets are reviewed in June so updates can be made prior to the beginning of the academic year (September). During the academic year, the Administrative Council meets biweekly, with a portion of each meeting devoted to evaluating the effectiveness of current activities.

As shown earlier, Figure 3.2 contains a list of strategic objectives and their associated action plans. To ensure goal performance levels for the first objective, achieving a high-quality student population, the Administrative Council has developed four major action plans: 1) continuing use of the Finley scholarship funds to attract top-level high school graduates, 2) increasing the level of contact with high school counselors and students, including on-campus visits by MCB administrators and admissions officers, 3) instituting MCB Listens, an anonymous web-based program designed to improve channels of student feedback, and 4) improving a curriculum alignment process to decrease the response time necessary for departments to introduce new material as environmental needs warrant.

To maintain a high-quality faculty, the strategic plan calls for enforcing the nine-hour instructional load (offered to faculty who are actively publishing their research) and increasing the level of faculty development (including support for professional development and incentive funds for rewarding high performance). This action plan will require stable state budgets and enhanced private funding. The overall human resource plan in support of the strategy to maintain a high-quality faculty ensures MCB retains these high-quality persons and, when needed, recruits high-quality replacements. The action plan includes 1) strong academic and/or professional credentials; 2) a recruiting process led by the chairs and faculty; 3) an orientation program for new faculty, with additional mentoring; 4) privately-funded faculty development funds, including summer research support; 5) funding for the purchase of instructional improvement materials; 6) an extended learning program; 7) the opportunity to participate in the Georgia State University Master Teachers Program; 8) special-topics training for all faculty and staff; 9) support for attendance at conferences and seminars; and 10) an evaluation process that provides incentives for strong teaching, research, and service performance.

To maintain adequate financial resources to support program excellence, the college must continue to work with the university's Office of Finance and Administration to effectively manage the state budgeting process and work more closely with the University Foundation and Dean's Leadership Council to increase the level of external program support, including scholarships, faculty endowments, and other strategic opportunities. These efforts include increased communications with alumni, who can play a major role in fundraising.

Finally, to build a market reputation consistent with program excellence, the strategic plan calls for 1) continued targeting of low performance areas on the EBI surveys in order to increase student and stakeholder satisfaction, 2) increasing student internships in order to build better relationships between students and their potential employers, 3) improving alumni contacts to enhance their role as college ambassadors in the marketplace, 4) improving employer contacts to increase opportunities for student placement, and 5) continuing support for MCB's director of external relations position and the associated initiatives in order to enhance marketplace visibility across all stakeholder groups.

Student, Stakeholder, and Market Focus

MCB is mission driven when targeting student segments and markets. The college pursued a mass-marketing strategy throughout the 1980s that included baccalaureate, master's, and doctoral student segments, both residential and distance delivery in scope. As it approached the 1990s, MCB made a significant strategic shift to its present focus on undergraduate-only business students, delivered in a residential format. The college now targets above-average students in the Rocky Mountain Region for its undergraduate business program and is the only AACSB-accredited business program in the area to have selected this key niche on which to focus 100% of its resources.

Within the undergraduate market, MCB has further differentiated between high school graduates, transfer students from other institutions (i.e., both community colleges and other four-year universities), and change-of-majors from within the university. MCB also makes its program available and attractive to nontraditional undergraduate students by offering a guaranteed evening schedule of all required general business courses.

Understanding Student Needs

The college uses a variety of methods to listen and learn about student and stakeholder requirements (see Figure 3.3). The methods include formal and informal channels and are categorized by segment. All students have an MCB-appointed individual faculty advisor. As students move through their degree program, they may select their own faculty advisor if they determine another faculty member is a better match for their career goals or their personality style.

Figure 3.3

Listening Methods for Students and Stakeholders at the Monfort College of Business

Group	Listening/Learning Methods
Prospective students and parents	• Preview Days sessions (10 events) • Junior Days sessions (2 events) • High school visits to MCB • Finley Fellows offers/communication • Individual student/parent visits to MCB • Faculty phone-calling program • MCB/UNC admissions office partnership
Current students	• Advising Center/deans office availability • Open-door practice • Small classes (contact with professors) • High student/faculty interaction • Faculty advisors/Advising Center • MCB student survey (spring) • EBI Student Satisfaction Survey (spring) • MCB course evaluations (each semester) • MCB Student Representative Council (monthly) • MCB Listens web site
Alumni/donors	• EBI Alumni surveys • Annual newsletter feedback page • Development meetings with dean • MCB/UNC Foundation/alumni partnership

Group	Listening/Learning Methods
Employers	• MCB Dean's Leadership Council interactions
	• MCB/UNC Career Services partnership
	• UNC career fairs and employer panels
	• Advisory board meetings feedback
	• Employer survey (annual)
	• AACSB meetings/seminars

Formal channels for assessing student needs and requirements include the use of three student surveys: 1) an internal student survey of all junior/senior students conducted at the beginning of each spring semester, 2) the EBI Student Satisfaction Survey administered to all graduating seniors, and 3) the student course evaluations conducted in every section of every course. Alumni surveys, placement rates, student council meetings, and advisory board discussions also provide additional feedback to the college.

Community college and high school representatives also visit MCB to exchange information regarding student expectations and requirements, and prospective students visit during Preview Days (for high school seniors) and Junior Days (for high school juniors) programs. The college also hosts students and teachers from specific high schools and offers a customized visit program tailored to individual school needs.

Informally, prospective students visit the college and engage in one-on-one discussions with faculty, staff, and/or deans. In 2003, faculty members phoned all prospective students who had been admitted but had not yet formally indicated they were going to attend, in order to attempt to answer questions and gain commitment. From such discussions, faculty members were able to identify the issues related to the students' enrollment decisions.

The college keeps listening and learning methods current with educational service needs and directions by relying on a number of methods, updating them as needed, and using technology when appropriate. When EBI benchmarking services became available, the college began using those services instead of relying solely on internal surveys. In addition, the college surveys a number of its segments on a regular basis to keep information current. AACSB keeps current on trends in business education, and MCB uses information from this organization.

Building Relationships With Students

The college uses several channels to build student relationships. In order to provide appropriate information to prospective students and their parents, the college works closely with those university admissions office personnel who visit regional high schools and community colleges. New students and their families participate in orientation sessions called Discover University of Northern Colorado. These sessions include presentations by the MCB dean and roundtable discussions with faculty members. Incoming students also learn about business course requirements and are advised on course selection.

Before arriving on campus, students are assigned a faculty advisor whom they can contact with any questions. Student professional organizations also exist for each business emphasis, and students are encouraged to join these clubs. Each student organization works with a faculty advisor, which also facilitates student/faculty interaction. The dean meets with the Student Representatives Council on a regular basis to help build college/student relationships.

The college also supports a number of traditional services for students as a means to increase satisfaction and retention. Services include a well-maintained study lounge, a cyber café with Internet/email connections, a snack/lunch room, convenient/affordable parking, and an email system. In addition, the university provides a full range of student support services.

Complaint Management

The college has a number of key access mechanisms for students and stakeholders to seek information, to pursue common purposes, and to make complaints. The college web site is a major access point for information. Other access points include the College Advising Center, faculty advisors, and departmental staff members. The student handbook (also available on the web site) outlines complaint and appeals processes for students. MCB follows the complaint management process outlined for students in the student handbook, for faculty in the Board Policy Manual, and for staff in the guidelines provided by the state of Colorado. The dean of students is available, if needed, as a liaison between students/parents and the university. There is a process for formal complaints that may result in a student taking his or her complaint to the university Academic Appeals Board. However, in the last decade only one complaint required this level of discussion to reach a resolution. The vast majority of complaints are solved by the people who are closest to the problem, such as a faculty member or department chair.

In 2003, MCB Listens, an electronic suggestion box, was implemented as a tool for tracking, measuring, reviewing, and evaluating complaints. The information from MCB Listens may be used by faculty governance committees as key inputs in their decision-making processes.

Student Satisfaction Determination

MCB uses several methods to determine student and stakeholder satisfaction. The EBI Student Survey given to graduating seniors provides a measure of overall satisfaction, as well as other measures of satisfaction, including quality of teaching, quality of teaching in major courses, integration of real-world concepts, practitioner interaction, social issues, ethics, technology, integration of international perspective, skill development experiences (written and oral communication), teamwork, and computer usage. The college also utilizes the EBI Faculty Satisfaction Survey, an internal MCB Student Survey conducted the first day of spring classes, and student evaluations administered at the end of every semester.

The data retrieved from these surveys are extremely pertinent to decisions made by the governance committees. Some of the data serve as trigger points to require action on a committee's part. Data are reviewed by the committees, which then make appropriate decisions and recommendations. Examples of recent decisions made based on satisfaction data include the hiring of a director of technology due to decreasing satisfaction with some aspects of technology and review of the instructional evaluation procedures due to decreasing faculty satisfaction in that area.

Measurement, Analysis, and Knowledge Management

MCB's mission, values, and strategic plan serve as the framework for establishing its KPIs. These KPIs are the primary performance measures for tracking overall organizational performance and for guiding daily operations (see Figure 3.4). Such information is utilized to develop strategies for improvement, allocate financial resources, assess performance, and evaluate the effectiveness of actions as conditions change.

Figure 3.4
Key Performance Indicators at the Monfort College of Business

- Quality of incoming freshmen students (average ACT)
- Quality of transfer students (average GPA)
- Student retention rates
- Business major counts
- MCB current student satisfaction (% recommending)
- Student learning in business (average overall ETS)
- High-touch curriculum (average class size)
- Quality of faculty (% academic or professional qualification)
- Quality of professional faculty (% professional qualification)
- Quality of academic faculty (assessment by exiting students)
- Faculty program satisfaction (average overall)
- Student satisfaction—facilities/computing resources
- Faculty satisfaction—computing resources
- Total available state funds (annual)
- Total available private funds (annual)
- Placement of graduates (% employed full-time)
- Exiting student satisfaction (average overall)
- Alumni satisfaction (average overall)
- Employer satisfaction (average overall)
- MCB press coverage (media coverage generated)

Performance Measurement

KPIs are selected and aligned to measure performance in meeting the college's mission, vision, and values. The KPIs are also aligned with the university's mission and the college's AACSB accreditation requirements. MCB's faculty governance groups and administration establish and implement plans to pursue the mission and values. These groups are also responsible for selecting the KPIs and other indicators, but the Administrative Council and dean oversee the final selection of performance indicators. Review groups for the KPIs include university administration, the Dean's Leadership Council, and faculty committees.

To support organizational decision-making and innovation, the student, faculty, and administrative governance groups, Dean's Leadership Council, and external constituencies examine the KPIs, other indicators, and comparative data on an ongoing basis. For some measures, the college has established performance triggers that will initiate further investigation should the measure fall below a specified level. For others, general trends and comparative data are reviewed and, if necessary, further investigation is initiated.

Performance data are used to make decisions for student admission, retention, and graduation requirements, for curriculum revisions, for faculty and staff performance evaluation, and for technology assessment. Scheduled reviews by the governance groups yield recommendations about program changes, policy matters, and changes in data requirements.

Use of Comparative Data

The college selects and ensures the effective use of key comparative data by selecting measures with the following characteristics: 1) determine how well the college is meeting its mission, 2) allow for comparative benchmarking against peer institutions, and 3) allow for the college to evaluate performance over an extended period of time.

The college incorporates best practices in business administration education into its mission and values. Some best practices are defined through the accreditation process, while others are defined through comparative analysis. For example, AACSB (2002-2003) released a report titled *Effective Practices: Undergraduate Career Services and Placement Offices*, which the college is currently using to assess its placement function. The leadership team recently toured the facilities of one of its key competitors to meet with its leadership and share best practices.

MCB has established a formal review schedule for the college's processes. This is separate from the review of comparative data and key indicators. Each academic year, a number of the processes are reviewed by senior leaders and the appropriate faculty groups to determine if they are effective and to determine where opportunities exist for further improvement. These processes aid in the selection and revision of KPIs and other indicators.

To ensure that performance measures are current with educational needs and directions, the college mission and values, all KPIs are 1) aligned with the AACSB accreditation standards and requirements; 2) reviewed on an ongoing basis by senior corporate managers (including the Dean's Leadership Council), alumni, and academic personnel; and 3) measured against data from external agencies (e.g., EBI, ETS) that invest in developing reliable, valid, and timely measures for management education. These three criteria provide a standard of currency and quality for MCB's KPIs and other indicators.

Performance Analysis

To perform an organizational review of the college, 20 KPIs are reviewed to assess the college's effectiveness in meeting its mission and values (shown earlier in Figure 3.4). These indicators encompass the four strategic goal areas, including student quality, faculty quality, financial stability, and program reputation. In all, several hundred satisfaction and performance measures are captured. The 20 KPIs represent the college's top tier, or vital few, measures in order to bring focus to the performance analysis.

The college's performance analyses are spread throughout its faculty governance and administrative structures. Each committee is charged with an annual set of activities pertaining to its domain that include performance reviews via analyses of a range of indicators. A number of the information sources, such as the EBI Student Satisfaction Survey, cut across multiple committee domains. The committees use a variety of tools, including trend analysis, benchmark comparisons, correlation analysis, and root cause analysis, to assist them in their performance reviews. All analyses eventually feed back into the Administrative Council. The dean then reviews the summaries of committee output and makes the final decisions on how to improve existing programs and processes.

Information and Knowledge Management

Data and information are made available through the web site, SEDONA, and a number of commercial and university reports. The college pursues a coordinated effort to review, capture, and maintain its data for quality management. MCB's Information Technology Services meets industry standards for security and reliability. The college has implemented a two-tier approach to managing technology. The university provides the college with the campus backbone and Internet access and technical support services. Since the university makes available reliable firewalls and security measures for the campus, the college gains a substantial improvement in service and security levels from this arrangement. Similarly, the purchase of technical support provides the college with services that it could not afford.

College technology planning is coordinated by the Technology Committee, a leadership group of faculty and technology staff. Funding for technology is stable and adequate, and is provided through three sources: 1) a business student technology fee, 2) an endowment program to support college technology, and 3) the general fund and tuition support. The combination of these sources provides resources to develop a vital technology environment.

Organizational Knowledge

Performance and satisfaction measures are made available in print, in magnetic media forms, and on the web site. The college also maintains a number of databases, with customized reporting available upon request. MCB acquires a wealth of demographic and enrollment data from the institutional research and planning and admissions offices and extracts data on an as-needed basis. Governance groups receive standard and individually tailored reports developed by the individual coordinators.

Best practices result from internal improvements arising from internal analysis and from outside influences, in particular from comparative data and AACSB. For example, admissions requirements for MCB are set to balance the likelihood of student success against faculty and physical resources and against the mission and values. The college is also sensitive to industry practices and uses focus groups, the Dean's Leadership Council, and the executive professor program to provide information on best practices.

Since MCB largely uses outside organizations for its performance and satisfaction data, the accuracy, reliability, and validity are established by these agencies. The validity and reliability of these instruments were an important part of the analysis that led to their selection.

The process for assessing satisfaction and performance is mature and established. The assessment program has been in place for more than 5 years with some aspects dating back 12 years. Over this period, revisions have been incorporated to improve the program, and the results have been used to make numerous program changes.

Faculty and Staff Focus

Empowered, data-driven departments manage the college's emphasis areas, while cross-functional committees manage the processes. All such groups operate within the strategy of high-touch, wide-tech, and professional depth and are committed to the mission of excellence within undergraduate business education. The work systems for the college include an organizational structure, new employee recruitment and orientation, professional development, performance evaluation, compensation, and recognition for superior achievement. Cooperation, initiative, and innovation are promoted through a departmental structure that is traditionally functional, and a faculty governance structure that is cross-functional in composition.

There are a total of 40 full-time employees in the college. Each academic department contains a faculty chair, a core of Ph.D.-qualified faculty, and an administrative staff person. A smaller number of executive professors and part-time adjunct professors are spread across the academic departments. Skill levels, resources, and experiences are very similar and equitably distributed across disciplines, with each department assigned equal professional development funds and budget per faculty member. All faculty have the same requirements with regard to academic/professional qualifications and instructional currency. The college maintains a hiring pool of qualified instructors who can be called on when an opening exists for which they are qualified. The hiring pool allows the college to maintain agility because of the ready pool of applicants that can be used to teach new or additional classes.

The shared governance structure is comprised of five standing cross-functional committees, which include committees for curriculum, faculty affairs, student affairs, technology, and the Administrative Council. To ensure cooperation, communication, and a balance of input, each committee has a representative from each academic area, and some have additional representatives, including students. Although each committee receives an annual charge from the dean, committees are encouraged to show initiative to address issues, problems, or concerns as the committee recognizes them, in order to maintain agility within the college.

Communication and skill sharing are accomplished through the governance structure where members from each department report issues and concerns to their departmental faculty and staff. Communication is enhanced through email, memos, faculty/staff meetings, newsletters, the web site, and SEDONA. The college is housed within a single building, and the logistical arrangement of having all faculty and administrative offices on one end of the facility enhances communication and skill sharing. Individual faculty offices are arranged in pods, with shared open space available within each pod.

Performance Management

Faculty annual evaluations provide feedback to faculty regarding their past performance and expectations of future performance. Comprehensive (i.e., post-tenure) reviews, conducted on a four-year cycle, provide feedback based on a longer time period. Merit pay is provided for high-performing faculty; one-third of the annual salary-raise pool is tied to merit performance for those who exceed stated expectations. Using private endowment funds, MCB instituted a program whereby high-performing staff members receive professional development funds that can be spent (with supervisor approval) on a range of seminars, software packages, or job-related technology equipment. These funds are awarded for research and service activities: $500 for each acceptable refereed journal publication and $1,000 for publications on a department's "Top 20 Journal List."

Faculty members are evaluated in three major performance areas: instruction, professional activity (scholarship), and service. To emphasize its mission on high-quality instruction, that component receives the highest weight of 45% of the evaluation. Professional activity and service are weighted at 35% and 20%, respectively, for the typical tenured/tenure-track faculty member. Weights are adjusted accordingly for administrators, with a reduced weight for instruction and an increased weight for service. Staff members also have three components within their annual evaluation system: customer service, administrative effectiveness, and technology skill development.

To ensure student opinions are an input for the evaluation system, student evaluations are a major source of information regarding teaching performance. At the department and college level, the Professor of the Year honor is awarded by students. The college's compensation, recognition, and reward practices reinforce high-performance work and a student and stakeholder focus through a variety of mechanisms including merit pay, faculty awards for teaching, research, and service, professional development funds for high-performing faculty and staff, named professorships, and summer grants for instructional improvement and research.

Hiring and Career Progression

Characteristics and skills required of potential staff are identified through the job description process in line with the guidelines of the State of Colorado for its classified employee system. Classified staff positions are arranged within a hierarchy based on level and type of job description, as well as experience level (i.e., years in grade). Classified staff may advance through the college ranks as opportunities arise, but may also choose to seek promotions elsewhere in the state's classified employee system if they so choose.

Faculty characteristics and skills are determined by the department faculty, chairs, and dean and are aligned with the curriculum. The department chair reviews the current cadre of faculty in his or her area and makes hiring recommendations based on the ability of candidates to address those curriculum areas that need additional depth. Tenure-track faculty are required to hold a terminal degree at the time of hire and

advance through the ranks based on productivity and performance quality in the areas of instruction, scholarship, and service. In general, at least 10 years of service are required to advance from the assistant to full professor rank.

Although state hiring regulations prohibit strict succession planning, the last two deans had previously served in the position of associate dean prior to their being hired into the top leadership position. Department chair positions are filled on a faculty rotation basis, with an initial three-year term renewable for one additional term. The promotion and tenure process helps provide effective career progression for professors. Tenure-track faculty undergo a mid-tenure review (during their third year of employment) to assess their progress toward tenure. The result is a decision on whether to continue that individual's employment throughout the full tenure process. Tenured faculty undergo a comprehensive review every four years.

Faculty certification is established at the time of hire, either by previous academic training (i.e., Ph.D.) or employment responsibility level and duration (i.e., executive). College policy requires that such certification be maintained and that each instructor maintain instructional currency. Faculty can maintain their currency through scholarly activity, professional activity, and professional service. Faculty who also maintain professional certifications must continue to meet the requirements mandated by their own external certification boards. Certified public accountants, for example, are required to earn a minimum of 40 continuing professional education credits annually to maintain their licensing.

Education, Training, and Development

Faculty and staff training and development contribute to the accomplishment of the college's mission and goals (see Figure 3.5). Faculty training helps keep faculty up to date as the educational environment continues to evolve. For example, as online course technology has advanced, the college has supported faculty development in this area through in-house training programs on commercial tools such as Blackboard, which is available to all faculty members on a university server. Attendance and presentations at professional conferences help faculty keep current within their field. Staff member training in areas such as technology skills and continuous improvement help individuals keep their own skill sets up-to-date and help prepare them for promotional opportunities.

The new employee orientation process for faculty helps individuals make an effective transition to the college environment. New faculty participate in two half-day sessions in which the deans, director of technology, and advising center personnel provide subject overviews on areas such as

Figure 3.5

Employee Education, Training, and Development at the Monfort College of Business

Purpose	Faculty	Staff
Career advancement	Training/experience required for promotion in rank	Training/experience required for advancement through state classified system
Development	Opportunities selected through annual evaluations	
Skill/knowledge needs	Tied to MCB strategic objectives and action plans in support of mission, vision, values, and culture	
Instructional currency	Professional development required to maintain currency in area(s) taught.	N/A
General skills/knowledge needs	Identified by department faculty by emphasis area; by appropriate governance group; by AACSB	Identified by supervisor; by State Personnel Employee Council
Technology training	Identified by department faculty by emphasis area; by Technology Committee	Identified by supervisor; by technology director
Continuous improvement	Required by AACSB; by NCA	Required by AACSB; by NCA

promotion and tenure guidelines, student advising tools, technology support systems for students and faculty, college history, strategic planning, curriculum development processes, and student admission, continuation, and graduation requirements. This formal program is supplemented through longer-term interaction with each new faculty member's department chair. College orientation and mentoring programs are preceded by a university program provided each fall semester.

Faculty and staff are given opportunities for ergonomic reviews performed by the Office of Environmental Health and Safety to help them create a better ergonomic work environment. The university's human resources office also conducts periodic training programs for all employees on issues such as sexual harassment and diversity training. Other campus groups, such as the university police and the Center for Professional Development, offer employees opportunities for continued training and education.

Education and training are delivered through a variety of methods. Software training is delivered on site with the testing at an off-site location. The Center for Professional Development and outreach training is delivered on campus. Education and training are also obtained through travel to professional conferences and AACSB meetings. External trainers are brought to campus in the areas of grant writing and negotiations. New faculty are mentored by experienced faculty in their discipline or by their department chair.

The use of new knowledge and skills on the job is reinforced through the performance evaluation process. Staff members use their technology training in the performance of their duties and often assist faculty with technology tasks within that staff person's domain of expertise. Annual staff evaluations take into account an individual's ability to effectively use the technology and professional development funds that are provided for outstanding performers. Faculty members are also rewarded through the annual evaluation process for the introduction of innovative teaching methods or significant applications of technology within the classroom.

MCB determines the key factors that affect faculty and staff well-being, satisfaction, and motivation through a variety of methods. Annual participation in the EBI Faculty Satisfaction Survey provides administrators with faculty data segmented by academic area, gender, and rank.

Periodic faculty meetings at the department and college level offer additional opportunities for administration to better understand faculty satisfaction levels and issues relative to performance motivation. The State Personnel Employee Executive Council is available as a listening post for MCB's administrative staff to use in evaluating campus issues. Staff may also discuss issues with their department chair or the dean.

Process Management

The college's educational programs and support processes are centered on creating a learning environment for preparing students for successful careers and responsible leadership in business. The college identifies and manages its key processes for creating student and stakeholder value and maximizing student learning and success using a variety of methods, but each is rooted in the fundamental principle of academic freedom. The college determines its learning-centered processes by utilizing its shared governance system.

Each governance committee uses the Plan-Do-Check-Act (PDCA) process to plan, control, and improve processes in its respective areas of responsibility, including processes for the areas of curriculum, technology, and faculty evaluation (see Figure 3.6). These processes have the greatest potential to create student and stakeholder value and impact the delivery of educational programs. The Curriculum Committee holds the major responsibility for managing the curriculum processes. The director of technology works with the Technology Committee to manage the college's technology processes, and the Administrative Council and Faculty Affairs Committee manage the faculty and staff evaluation processes. The key learning-centered processes, their key requirements, and the assessment measures for each process are shown in Figure 3.7.

The meeting of curriculum objectives is facilitated through the course syllabi, which are reviewed annually by department chairs. These course information documents reinforce the curriculum objectives by stating how ethical, global, technology, and communication issues will be covered. The Curriculum Committee follows an extensive review process for the college's curriculum, in addition to using university program reviews and AACSB evaluation cycles.

Figure 3.6
The Plan-Do-Check-Act Cycle for Process Improvement at the Monfort College of Business

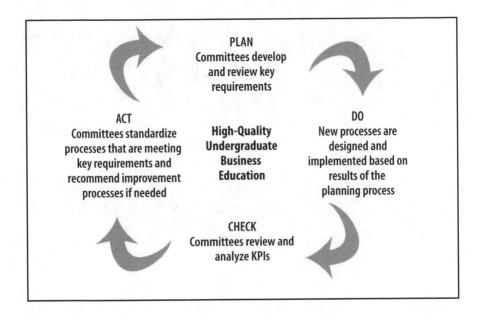

Technology is interwoven throughout classes and is a part of the college's wide-technology strategy. The purpose of the Technology Committee is to serve as an intracollege communications network to disseminate information regarding technology and to serve as the primary technology planning group for the college. A primary goal of the committee is to anticipate the technology environment that students will be likely to experience on the job following graduation. The Technology Committee develops the technology plan and reviews the effectiveness of current technology.

The college uses a number of different educational delivery processes that are appropriate to the type and level of the class. Many courses, especially at the higher level, are designed to provide hands-on learning. Examples of these classes include the Student Alumni Foundation Fund class, where students manage a University Foundation portfolio worth approximately $1 million; the Small Business Counseling class, in which students serve as consultants for area businesses; the Marketing Research class, which conducts marketing research projects for area businesses such

Figure 3.7
Key Learning-Centered Processes, Requirements, and Measures at the Monfort College of Business

Learning-Centered Processes	Key Process Requirements	In-Process Measures	Measures
Curriculum	Introduce students to contemporary business knowledge and practice.	• Review of course syllabi	• ETS exam results
	Provide students with a broad understanding of the functional areas of business.	• Review of course syllabi	• ETS exam results
	Prepare students to recognize ethical dilemmas and to make ethical business decisions.	• Minutes of coverage in core by ethical topic • Review of course syllabi by each department	• EBI UG Business Exit Study • ETS exam results
	Prepare students to address the unique issues of competing in a global business environment.	• Minutes of coverage in core by global topic • Review of course syllabi by each department	• EBI UG Business Exit Study • ETS exam results
	Prepare students to use oral/written communication skills in a business environment.	• Amount and types of oral communication in core • Review of course syllabi by each department	• EBI UG Business Exit Study

Learning-Centered Processes	Key Process Requirements	In-Process Measures	Measures
	Prepare students with the knowledge of business technology and the opportunity for application.	• Amount and types of technology usage in core • Review of course syllabi by each department	• EBI UG Business Exit Study • EBI Alumni Survey
	Introduce students to business information resources and their application.	• Amount and types of information resources usage in core • Review of course syllabi by each department	• EBI UG Business Exit Study
	Prepare students to work in a demographically diverse business environment.	• Amount and types of diversity coverage in core • Review of course syllabi by each department	• ETS exam results
Technology	Provide students with access to a broad array of existing and emerging business technologies.	• Upgrade/replace schedule in student labs, classrooms, and offices	• EBI UG Business Exit Study • EBI Faculty Study
Faculty Evaluation	Ensure faculty are academically and/or professionally qualified.	• Amount and types of intellectual contributions (i.e., refereed works)	• % academically or professionally qualified

as State Farm's regional office; and the Direct Marketing class, which develops a ready-to-implement strategy each year for a national client such as the *New York Times* or Toyota.

The college does offer a very limited number of online courses to meet the requirements of a degree program administrated through one of its partner colleges on the university campus. In general, distance learning is used to enhance rather than replace the college's residential programs. For example, distance technology was used to bring two notable guest speakers into the MCB classroom: Harvey Pitt, one week prior to his stepping down as chair of the United States Securities and Exchange Commission, and Michael Oxley (R-Ohio), cosponsor of the Sarbanes-Oxley Act on corporate accountability.

These continuous improvement processes create value for students and other key stakeholders by providing current knowledge and skills to students, increasing the reputation of the college as it receives recognition for graduating students who are prepared for employment, providing increased opportunities for student-faculty interaction, and providing a number of well-qualified business professionals for the state of Colorado, given that 80% of the college's graduates remain in Colorado.

Assessment of Student Learning

The key performance measures or indicators used for the control and improvement of MCB's learning-centered processes may be divided into four groups: 1) formative by course, 2) summative by course, 3) formative by emphasis, and 4) summative by emphasis. Formative indicators by course include exams, the enforcement of prerequisites, and course assignments. The summative by course indicators are the final grades assigned by the professor and his or her course evaluations. The formative by emphasis indicators include internship reports, advising, and grade point average requirements. The summative indicators by emphasis include emphasis GPAs, ETS exam results, student performance in the capstone courses, graduation requirements, and results of the alumni survey.

The college uses a variety of methods to improve its learning-centered processes so student success can be maximized and educational programs, offerings, and services can be improved. External feedback mechanisms include alumni surveys, student surveys, ETS exam results, input from advisory boards, and its meeting of AACSB guidelines and standards. Internal review mechanisms include a comprehensive program review of MCB conducted every five years, regular meetings of the responsible governance committees, program changes initiated at the department level, and annual reviews of course prerequisites, course syllabi, catalog requirements, and course descriptions.

Reference

Association to Advance Collegiate Schools of Business. (2002–2003). *Effective practices: Undergraduate career services and placement offices.* St. Louis, MO: Author.

Note

Six months after this chapter was written the Monfort College of Business at the University of Northern Colorado received the Malcolm Baldrige National Quality Award in November 2004.

4

New Mexico State University–Carlsbad

Rick S. Blackburn

New Mexico State University–Carlsbad (NMSU–C), New Mexico's first community college, was established in 1950. Located in southeastern New Mexico, it is a branch of New Mexico's land-grant college, New Mexico State University–Las Cruces. It is an open-door community college that accepts all students regardless of their level of academic preparedness and provides them with the opportunity to achieve their educational and career goals. NMSU–C enrolls approximately 1,250 students each semester and has been involved in quality improvement initiatives since 1994. The mission, core values, and vision of NMSU–C embrace the educational criteria of the Malcolm Baldrige Award. The entire campus community helped develop the vision statement, which includes such linkages to the Malcolm Baldrige criteria as valuing and fostering learner-centered education, continuous improvement and organizational learning, and valuing students, faculty, staff, and other stakeholders.

Leadership Systems

New Mexico State University–Carlsbad (NMSU–C) has aligned the university's leadership system and all critical campus systems with the Baldrige quality framework (see Figure 4.1). The campus executive officer, the campus academic officer, the campus student services officer, and the campus finance officer compose the Campus Executive Committee (CEC). This senior leadership team guides institutional planning and assessment, fiscal management, resource utilization, and mission attainment. Relying on input from students, faculty, staff, and external stakeholders, these senior leaders develop values, directions, and expectations and then deploy these elements throughout the campus community. Mid-level leaders implement the committee's directives.

The campus executive officer deploys the mission, core values, and performance expectations through the Leadership System, the Strategic Planning System, and the Human Resources System, and the chief academic officer deploys these processes through four division coordinators, who represent the 30 full-time and 75 part-time faculty. The campus student service officer oversees student service units, and the chief financial officer is responsible for deployment of the fiscal management system, the facilities management system, and the information system.

Senior leaders deploy the university's mission, core values, and performance expectations in accordance with the school's link to its core values of leadership, long-range outlook, valuing employees, continuous improvement, organizational learning, fast response, results orientation, and management by fact. Campus leadership communicates these values, goals, and expectations in a variety of formats including the university web site, new employee orientation materials, new student orientation materials, graduate outcomes for students, town hall meetings (all employees), and electronic communication.

Governance Structure

The campus governance system facilitates interaction among all stakeholders; the formal shared governance structure consists of a steering committee and seven standing committees. A steering committee, composed of the chairs of the seven standing committees and the campus executive officer (an ex-officio member), meets on a monthly basis. Each standing committee is composed of members of the faculty, the classified staff, the administration, and the student body and at least one (ex-officio) member of the Campus Executive Council. There are seven standing commit-

Figure 4.1

The Organizational Performance System at New Mexico State University–Carlsbad

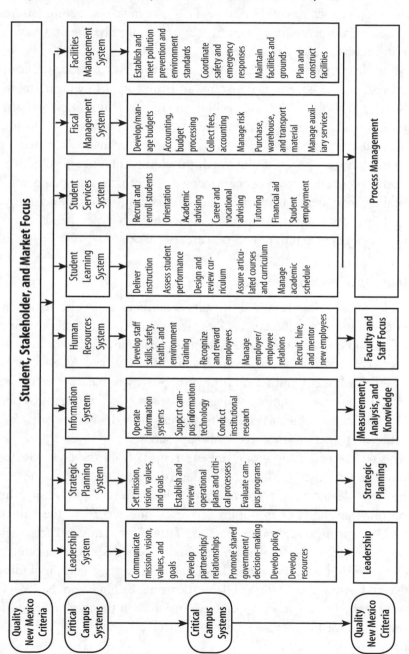

tees: Institutional Planning and Assessment, Faculty Interests, Support and Staff Interests, Academic Interests, Student Interests, Instructional Resources, and Facilities and Security. This governance structure ensures that the entire university community can propose change and have a voice in decision-making processes.

Senior leaders foster legal and ethical behavior throughout the leadership system, the governance system, and the campus by clearly communicating school policies and regulations to all faculty, staff, and students. Communication is accomplished by several methods: publishing the student code of conduct, providing online policy manuals, providing an online business procedure manual, providing guidance through the mentoring program, providing open access to all programs, encouraging a cultural diversity component in all course syllabi, providing awareness of cultural diversity and diverse learning styles through Title V, and providing workshops designed to promote awareness of others.

Organizational Performance Review

Senior leaders regularly review the results of annual assessments that measure organizational performance. Key assessment tools include the Student Opinion Survey to measure student satisfaction, the Adult Learner Needs Survey to measure student needs, and the Personal Assessment of College Environment and Campus Quality Survey to measure employee satisfaction. The Community Satisfaction Survey is used to measure community satisfaction. All survey results are also shared with students, faculty, staff, and external stakeholders as appropriate.

The senior leadership group reviews reports from the New Mexico Commission on Higher Education to determine cohort success, reports to the New Mexico State Department of Education on Adult Basic Education programs and Perkins Grant activities, and reports to the United States Department of Education tracking Title V programs and activities. Senior leaders examine feedback from Quality New Mexico applications, Baldrige applications, and reports from accrediting agencies, including the North Central Association's Higher Learning Commission. NMSU–C was one of the first six schools in the country to join the Academic Quality Improvement Program, a Baldrige-inspired alternative to traditional accreditation processes.

If, as a result of these ongoing performance reviews, senior leaders determine that goals or strategies need to be revised, those revisions are integrated into the strategy development process implementation, specifically the "outcomes" and "results" components. Two examples of recent review findings and the opportunities they generated are described below.

- **Example 1.** *Finding: An analysis of enrollment data showed that fall-to-fall retention data for first-time, full-time students had markedly decreased.* To improve retention, the university researched alternatives and made the following recommendations:

  ~ Require first-time, full-time students to enroll in College 101, "College Life/Success"

  ~ Improve the placement of students into appropriate courses through a more rigorous check of prerequisites

  ~ Improve placement testing in key subject areas

  ~ Create support courses in English and math

  ~ Teach advisors to use student tracking software

- **Example 2.** *Finding: Graduation data suggested that the retention rate for Hispanics was lower than for non-Hispanics.* To close the gap, senior leaders incorporated these data into a federal grant application (Title V–"Strengthening Hispanic Institutions"), which was approved for a five-year, $1.9 million award. Using the grant award, the university was able to take needed actions:

  ~ Provide faculty members with release time to develop English and math courses that would specifically address the needs of a multicultural classroom of students with different learning styles

  ~ Send tutors and teachers to conferences on teaching in a culturally diverse classroom

  ~ Sponsor workshops designed to help faculty and staff teach and retain at-risk students

Support of Key Communities

NMSU–C provides its service area, defined as Eddy County and Southeast New Mexico, with higher education, customized training programs, and self-enrichment courses. The Citizens' Professional Advisory Committee structure allows the university to anticipate and respond to community needs and concerns. Local employers, local agencies, alumni, students, elected officials, and other community members are represented on these committees, which meet formally at least twice a year. Members are encouraged to suggest new programs, recommend revisions to existing programs, and evaluate all campus outcomes. For example, in response to demand from area educators, senior campus leaders facilitated the implementation of new degree programs, including a four-year degree in elementary education, a master's degree in education, and a doctorate in community college leadership.

NMSU–C leadership encourages campus employees to strengthen key communities by including community involvement in job descriptions for faculty and staff positions and by rewarding outstanding community service as part of the faculty annual review process. The campus leadership leads by example in this area. For example, the campus executive officer serves on the board of directors of the New Mexico Endowment for the Humanities. Faculty and staff members select the key communities they wish to serve. Presently, 97% of university employees serve on one or more community groups.

NMSU–C has also demonstrated leadership in improving the environment for the campus and the surrounding community. The university has received three recognitions from the Green Zia award program of the New Mexico Department of Environment. The Green Zia Environmental Excellence Program is a state recognition program that acknowledges organizations that have taken strides to improve immediate and long-term environmental conditions. NMSU–C is the first educational institution to be so recognized.

Strategic Planning

NMSU–C, a branch campus of New Mexico State University, the state's land-grant, doctoral-granting, research university, is independently accredited and independently funded through a legislated formula appropriation, tuition and fees, and mill levies. The legislated formula is based on credit hours generated through enrollment and headcount of enrollment from an identified prior year. Policies and procedures are primarily driven by the university's relationship with the parent campus.

NMSU–C defines itself as an "open-door, comprehensive community college," and thus its mission, vision, and core values frequently differ from those of the parent campus. Programs such as developmental studies and adult basic education have no counterpart on the parent campus. The presence of these programs at NMSU–C exemplifies the college's local community focus and requires a Strategy Development Process that differentiates the branch campus at Carlsbad from the parent campus.

NMSU–C develops and sustains five strategic plans: 1) five-year plan, 2) three-year technology plan, 3) marketing plan, 4) student retention plan, and 5) physical plant upgrades plan. These five campus-wide plans and their annual revisions drive the overall planning process. Annual revisions may include updating goals and objectives; implementing new initiatives in teaching, research, and service; revising, adding, and deleting programs or services; managing enrollments; and assessing learner and program outcomes.

A critical component in measuring student learning outcomes is the campus assessment process, the conceptual framework of which is linked to NMSU–C's mission, graduate outcomes, and planning processes. The strategic planning process encompasses institutional assessment data, program outcomes data, and course data. Student information including placement scores, retention, and progress toward degree, provides the campus with longitudinal data to guide planning, strategy development, and decision-making.

Strategy Development

NMSU–C's Strategic Planning Process begins with the collection and distribution of relevant demographic, operational, and survey data to campus personnel and other stakeholders (see Figure 4.2). The analyses of these data drive the overall projections for operations and identify areas for improvement and growth. Concurrently, each area develops multiyear projections and plans. The CEC reviews the plans and data in order to develop goals and action priorities for the institution.

Figure 4.2
The Strategy Development Process at New Mexico State University–Carlsbad

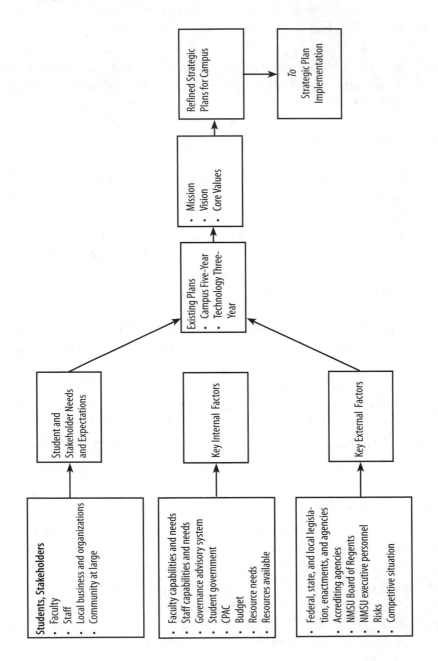

The mission, vision, and core values drive the campus strategy development process. The strategy development process for student and stakeholder needs and expectations relies on surveys, input from the campus governance system, feedback on the long-term planning process, program reviews, enrollment and graduation rates, and other relevant measures. The revision process includes analyses of current demographic and economic trends in the service area. Plan projections consider the community's college attendance rates and the projected number of high school graduates who will select NMSU–C. Each administrative unit develops goals and sets objectives, and the CEC then defines a realistic menu of projects.

Strategic Objectives

NMSU–C incorporates key strategic long-term objectives into three-year and five-year development plans. Twelve recent objectives were formulated.

- Establish a student database for advising and tracking students by 2005

- Incorporate competency-based instruction in all developmental classes by 2005

- Implement a teaching technology lab by fall 2004

- Identify and purchase an educational administration software package by 2006

- Renew accreditation using the Academic Quality Improvement Program standards by 2006

- Increase student college enrollment by 2% annually through 2006

- Increase the rate of minority student enrollment by 20% by 2006

- Increase enrollment of students from outlying service community areas by 15% by 2006

- Improve student retention by 2%–5% annually through 2006

- Improve minority retention by 2%–5% annually through 2006

- Increase degree completion of Hispanic students to 33% by 2006

- Design, plan, and fund a fine arts program and building by 2006

These short- and long-term objectives respond to the identified needs of stakeholders and are further shaped by budgetary considerations; faculty, staff, and operational capabilities; and available resources. Assessment of the success of these objectives will be made internally and will be based on best practices by the respective areas of responsibility.

Action Plans

Data analyses identify key short-term action plans. Most short-term action plans result from data about stakeholder satisfaction. As a result of, and in conjunction with, the strategy development process and the strategic plan implementation process, senior leaders define a realistic menu of projects, which are then translated into key long-term action plans. Short-term action plans address improvement opportunities identified through student survey feedback, student feedback from faculty evaluations, employee survey feedback, and community satisfaction results. Long-term action plans address elements of the five-year campus plan, the three-year technology plan, the Title V grant, and institutional reaccreditation activities (see Figure 4.3).

The allocation of campus resources is primarily a budgetary process. Each spring, all areas of campus are solicited for input about projects and budgets for the next academic year. Additional methods of resource allocation are undertaken at various management-level meetings, which are held regularly to make mid-course adjustments in the submitted budgets. Resources are allocated according to priorities that parallel the priorities within the action plan and action plan sub-units. All education and service areas participate in establishing priorities and resource allocations.

Student, Stakeholder, and Market Focus

Of the approximately 1,250 students NMSU–C enrolls each semester, 75% or more test initially into at least one developmental course; many

Figure 4.3
Sample Action Plans and Indicators Used by New Mexico State University–Carlsbad

Sample Action Plan Components	Examples of Measures and Indicators
Feedback from ALNS survey on what students need	Comparison of results from subsequent ALNS survey
PACE & CQS survey results on how to improve the campus	Comparison of results from subsequent PACE survey
Community Satisfaction Survey results on how to better serve the community	Comparison of results from subsequent Community Satisfaction Survey
Elements of five-year campus plan	Completion of identified milestones and annual review, monitoring, and modification of planned activities through the strategic planning processes
Elements of three-year technology plan	Completion of identified milestones and annual review, monitoring, and modification of planned activities through the strategic planning processes
Elements of Title V grant	Completion of identified milestones and annual review, monitoring, and modification of planned activities through the strategic planning processes
Elements of NCA AQIP quality-based accreditation activity	Feedback from NCA and completion of identified milestones and annual review, monitoring, and modification of planned activities through the strategic planning processes

are single parents; 35% are Hispanic; most work full- or part-time. All of these factors are indicative of possible at-risk students, whose success can be ensured only through highly individualized advisement and instruction, a supportive and nurturing academic and social environment, and enough institutional flexibility to respond rapidly to perceived needs. Enrollment has grown dramatically each decade, requiring NMSU–C to rapidly expand programs and services to provide access to interested students (see Figure 4.4).

The campus provides a variety of educational opportunities to its students and to community members. Eddy County's Adult Basic Education program is housed on campus, providing basic English, reading, and mathematics instruction for students preparing to take GED tests. The student services office provides information and counseling for those successful

Figure 4.4
Enrollment Growth at New Mexico State University–Carlsbad

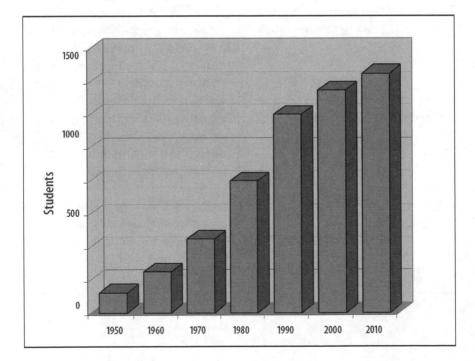

completers of the GED who wish to enroll in college classes. Additionally, the college offers a sequence of developmental studies classes in English, math, and reading, which are designed to prepare students academically for college-level courses. Careful pre-enrollment testing tries to ensure accurate placement of students into these sequences or into freshman-level courses.

There are 22 certificate programs (30 to 36 credit hours) designed to prepare students to enter the workplace with marketable skills; 12 associate of arts degree programs, designed to prepare students to transfer into baccalaureate degree-granting institutions; 16 associate of applied science degree programs, which prepare students to enter the workforce upon graduation; and 15 transfer programs, which offer freshman- and sophomore-level courses for students planning to transfer to baccalaureate institutions. The community services department offers noncredit educational classes, courses of personal interest, and enrichment programs for students of all ages. NMSU–C also hosts the regional Small Business Development Center and the Manufacturing Sector Development programs.

The mission of the campus is to provide access to higher education. To accomplish this mission, the campus aggressively seeks feedback from students, employees, the local community, employers, local school districts, transfer institutions, and agencies. Census data, Chamber of Commerce data, and community survey data are reviewed. For example, the Adult Basic Education program conducted a comprehensive community needs assessment in April 2002, which indicated that 38% of respondents had less than a high school education. A focus group composed of students provides a continuing source of information to the marketing research team, which uses that information to refine both its research and marketing approaches.

Determining Student and Stakeholder Needs

NMSU–C uses multiple overlapping methods for determining student needs, interests, and expectations. These methods focus primarily on student interests and demographics. The college application process initiates direct methods of determining student needs and interests. A required placement test, which begins with a survey of personal and support needs, is the second method of identifying student needs. The placement test also provides specific information about student proficiency levels in math,

English, and reading. Registration is the third opportunity for directly determining student needs. Students may enroll full-time or part-time and choose morning, afternoon, or evening courses.

The campus annually administers the ACT Student Opinion Survey and triennially the ACT Adult Learners Needs Assessment, both of which are nationally normative surveys. The Student Opinion Survey assesses the needs and characteristics of students and student satisfaction with programs and services. Generally, the response rate is 45% to 50%, exceeding the national response rate of approximately 30%. The college also has access to comparative data from the four other New Mexico schools that participate in the survey and from all schools with a student population of 500 to 1,500 students. These data provide clear standards for comparing student needs and interests with those of students at other two-year colleges.

Student information and survey results are analyzed, distributed, reviewed by faculty, staff, and campus leadership, and the results are compared to established goals and measures of performance. Actionable results are integrated into NMSU–C's planning process. Direct consultation with students, use rates of campus-provided services, student focus groups, information from student government, student demand for courses, and contributions to suggestion boxes all help to determine student needs. The campus's governance system committees also include student representatives, thus providing students with a direct voice in the college governance system and the college with valuable input from students.

Anticipating Future Student Needs

Anticipated changes in needs and future student expectations are integrated into planning through the strategy development and strategic plan implementation processes. Current trends in education and employment are tracked through campus reviews and through dialogues with community members, civic leaders, representatives from business and industry, and other stakeholders. Projections are based on analyses of enrollment trends and local economic factors.

Demographic data and information about issues that may impact future enrollment trends are derived from partnership activities with Carlsbad, Loving, and Artesia K–12 school districts and dialogues with district officials. To determine enrollment trends, leadership analyzes, semester-by-semester, such data as FTE numbers, headcounts, numbers and types of first-time students, and numbers of continuing students, using these data to strengthen enrollment.

Demographic data collected on current students provides campus staff with knowledge of future students. Campus-sponsored activities such as Career Day, where admissions personnel visit local high schools, also offer valuable insight into the profiles of future students. The annual high school principals and counselors luncheon is an opportunity for college staff members to interact with feeder school administrators. Campus leadership engages in discussions with the Chamber of Commerce to learn about potential changes in the area's economic base and determine the effect that such changes will have on enrollment.

Other means for identifying changing expectations and needs of future graduates include college representation at trade shows and professional conferences that are designed to apprise academic programs of new developments in particular industries, of the requirements of employers, and of new trends in various career fields. Forums with area leaders in business and industry, such as the semiannual meetings with NMSU–C's Citizens Professional Advisory Committees, provide similar but more localized information about the kind of education that will make graduates valuable to area employers.

Legislative initiatives, such as New Mexico lottery scholarships, welfare reform, accountability standards, and reimbursement formula, affect access and compliance requirements for students as well as operational mandates for NMSU–C. Periodic reauthorization of federal financial aid and other aid programs considerably influences future enrollments. As guidelines change, college staff must be responsive to student needs and have a presence in the community and in local high schools to interpret the new guidelines for students and parents.

To be responsive to the needs of future students, including initiating new programs or eliminating outdated programs, campus leadership analyzes information about students and develops actionable plans. For example, students take placement tests upon admission. Approximately 75% of students test at the remedial level. In response to these findings, the college developed a student success model, which consists of strategies to help student services, the Learning Assistance Center, and job placement and career counseling to effectively serve students. Individual educational action plans are also developed to help students make academically sound decisions about completing their educational goals.

Communicating With Students and Stakeholders

NMSU–C recognizes that effective student and stakeholder relationships are critical to the well-being of the campus and its future. Student and stakeholder needs, expectations, and levels of satisfaction are analyzed and the results incorporated into the strategy development process to enhance the delivery of services. The college uses several indicators to measure key stakeholder relationships. Responses to evaluations of activities involving key stakeholders indicate positive responses to the college's efforts to maintain effective working relationships.

The term "stakeholder" refers to both external and internal stakeholders. NMSU–C maintains effective relationships with key stakeholders to support and enhance its ability to improve its services. The campus has strong associations with the local community, employers, K–12 school districts, transfer institutions, and state and federal agencies. Varieties of methods are used to determine stakeholder needs, some formal and others informal. Formal methods include review of and compliance with legislative mandates determined by initiatives, review of local demographic data, articulation agreements, program reviews, accreditation, reports, and ongoing as well as targeted surveys. Informal methods include feedback from advisory committees, partnership activities, conferences, and outreach activities.

NMSU–C's approach to effective relationships with students is to emphasize the availability of well-prepared staff to answer all questions and address all needs. The student population at NMSU–C is predominantly first-generation students, who need and appreciate personal interaction with staff. College 101, a required class for all new students and taught by faculty and staff, provides students with immediate access to the student services staff member or faculty member who both teaches the class and acts as the student's mentor through the first semester. National studies show that new students who feel connected to their school or to a professional staff member are more likely to succeed than students who feel anonymous.

NMSU–C maintains numerous other relationships with schools and organizations within its area of influence. For example, NMSU–C maintains articulation and service agreements with NMSU–Las Cruces, which allows the parent school to offer degree sequences using NMSU–C facilities. Many Eddy County residents are geographically and economically bound. NMSU–C's ITV and other technologies provide educational opportunities not otherwise possible for students. NMSU–C also offers manufacturing programs to Eddy County residents and has formed alliances with School-to-Work, the State of New Mexico, the Rural Community College Initiative, and Eastern New Mexico University–Roswell to assist in economic and educational opportunities for rural residents.

Students have formal and informal channels to comment, air complaints, and file grievances with faculty, staff, and administrators. College policies, described in the college catalog and the student handbook, detail the procedures for filing complaints and grievances. Comment cards may be submitted directly to the CEC, a system that keeps upper-level administrators abreast of student concerns.

The complaint management process handles both formal and informal complaints. After the nature of the complaint is determined, the complaint is assigned to the appropriate campus leader for investigation and resolution. Students are informed of the grievance and complaint policy during orientation, and it is reinforced in writing in the student handbook and the campus catalog. Complaints are discussed at executive team meetings and at departmental meetings. It is then the responsibility of the appropriate senior campus leader to remedy the problem.

Determining Student and Stakeholder Satisfaction

The campus uses a number of methods to determine student and stakeholder satisfaction (see Figure 4.5). However, the primary method for determining student satisfaction at NMSU–C is the ACT Student Opinion Survey. This survey was selected after a campus committee reviewed all available normed instruments that address satisfaction in higher education. The committee chose the Student Opinion Survey because its normative base is composed of community college students, because the services it surveys most closely match the services offered at NMSU–C, and because it is the most frequently used satisfaction survey instrument in community colleges.

Figure 4.5
Methods for Determining Student and Stakeholder Satisfaction at
New Mexico State University–Carlsbad

Stakeholders Satisfaction Determination	Students	Key Stakeholders (Campus Employees)	Key Stakeholders (CPAC, Community Groups)
Determination Processes	• ACT Student Opinion Survey (SOS) • ACT Adult Learner Needs Survey (ALNS) • ABE Student Satisfaction Survey	• PACE survey • CQS survey	• Internal Community Satisfaction Survey (CSS)
Measurement Scales and Data	• SOS—national normative data measures • ALNS—national normative data measures • ABE—internal survey, multiyear comparisons	• PACE—national normative data • CQS—national normative data	• Internal instrument for community assessment
Objectivity	• Administered in classrooms • Students remain anonymous	• Administered on campus • Respondents remain anonymous	• Administered at meetings: CPAC, service clubs, and Interagency Council

Stakeholders Satisfaction Determination	Students	Key Stakeholders (Campus Employees)	Key Stakeholders (CPAC, Community Groups)
Satisfaction Measures	• SOS—multiple indirect measures, direct measures—overall rating • ALNS—multiple measures of needs, instrument assesses student needs only • ABE—satisfaction determination	• PACE Indirect—62 items organized into 7 factors • CQS Indirect—89 items, 9 local items (new 2002)	• Direct measure overall rating
Capture Actionable	• SOS—compare data, comparable school trends • ALNS—compare data, student needs • ABE—compare past data	• Compare past data with comparable schools • Compare data with comparable schools	• CS—future data with past data
Follow-up for Interaction, Feedback	• SOS-ALN—campus-wide sharing of results, correct deficit issues, action plans to improve results • ABE—ABE program use	• Campus-wide sharing of results, development of action plans for improvement of lowest scores	• Campus-wide sharing, critical areas
Satisfaction Relative to Comparable Schools	• SOS—500+ schools nationally Segmented data • ALNS—100+ schools nationally • ABE—internal instrument	• PACE—60+ schools nationally • CQS—125+ schools nationally	• Internal instrument, limited comparative data available

Measurement, Analysis, and Knowledge Management

At all institutional levels, data are selected according to whether they meet specific requirements.

- Data are subject to measurable and relevant performance criteria

- Data are reliable

- Data can be analyzed within a meaningful timeframe

- Data can be collected with available resources (technology and personnel)

- Data can provide valid, ongoing, and actionable information

These data include student/stakeholder feedback and NMSU branch, state, regional, and national data.

The CEC meets weekly to discuss operational progress, performance measures, budgets, and goals, using the most recent data. Resources and plans may be redirected and modified in response to new data to ensure that daily operations and organizational performance are maintained. Information is disseminated monthly to the campus, monthly through town hall meetings and the Campus Connection, and daily as needed through emails and special meetings of governance committees.

Performance Analysis

Data collection, review, analysis, planning, and implementation are continual processes at NMSU–C. Campus leadership relies on several factors: campus performance history, internal data, and data provided by NMSU–Las Cruces, the State Department of Education, the Commission on Higher Education, the New Mexico Association of Community Colleges, and other sources. National data, survey data, and data from shared information arrangements within the North Central Association Academic Quality Improvement Program (AQIP) schools allow NMSU–C to compare its operational performance to that of similar two-year schools and thus identify and replicate best practices that may align and improve organizational performance.

Priorities for information and data are driven by needs that emerge in the strategic planning process. The comparative evaluation of planning processes, key processes, action plans, and opportunities for improvement are driven by the available data. Campus leadership identifies key school processes that afford meaningful data collection and informative comparisons. Where state and national data are available, comparative performance is evaluated. Key action plans are developed, incorporating expectation data, which include timelines, landmarks, and performance goals. Opportunities for improvement are based on the results of comparative evaluation of campus performance with available data.

NMSU–C relies heavily on meaningful comparative data obtained from such national sources as ASSET (student placement tests), Personal Assessment of College Environment Surveys, Campus Quality Surveys, National Council Licensure Exams, Student Opinion Surveys, Adult Learner Needs Surveys, and the America Association of Community Colleges. State sources include New Mexico's Commission on Higher Education, the State Department of Education, New Mexico's Association of Community Colleges, and NMSU branch campuses. Other sources of comparative data include NMSU–C's past performance data, feedback from the campus planning process, and information derived from AQIP members.

Data from performance measures are reviewed and assessed in conjunction with capabilities, changing needs of stakeholders, priority initiatives, and opportunities for innovation. Results, findings, and conclusions are circulated among the various leadership groups and standing committees and their inputs solicited. These inputs are generated through a combination of primary and secondary research collected both formally and informally. Primary data are gathered from campus sources, from the parent campus at Las Cruces, and from external sources. The campus community considers the fiscal implications of improvement and the correlation of data in the planning process.

Information Management

Critical data are available to faculty and staff to support the operational effectiveness of the campus. NMSU–Las Cruces maintains all student data from NMSU–C. The parent campus also maintains relevant data for personnel, payroll, purchasing, and other records. These data are available online with appropriate user permissions. For example, full-time faculty may access student data from their office computers. Student data are also available to all appropriate administrative and support personnel. Selected administrative employees and CEC members may access personnel and payroll databanks.

The campus planning and budgetary processes focus on regularly scheduled replacement of computer hardware and upgrading of software. NMSU–C maintains master educational user licensing, which enables the campus to equip student computer labs with the most recent software. The campus computer help desk immediately responds to major hardware or software problems and upgrades equipment and software on a priority basis. NMSU–C's staff relies on NMSU–Las Cruces to maintain current configurations in their databanks. NMSU–C supplements Las Cruces student data with local software such as Student Space, a student advising and tracking tool that focuses on data needs of community colleges in New Mexico.

Faculty and Staff Focus

NMSU–C designs, organizes, and manages work assignments for faculty and staff through a work system classification structure that divides full-time employees into three categories: faculty, administrative staff, and classified staff. NMSU–C also relies on part-time college instructors, teachers, temporary workers, and student employees. Delegation of authority, recognition of excellence, provision of work-area autonomy, and inclusion in decision-making promote cooperation, collaboration, initiative, innovation, and flexibility among all groups. All employee categories are represented on almost all committees, an organizational strategy that greatly facilitates communication among employee groups.

The design, management, and improvement of work processes that support campus action plans are a direct function of campus leadership and the result of strategic planning integrated with the critical campus processes. The focus of faculty and staff resource plans is on student needs and student success. Administrative and classified staff work processes also focus on student and stakeholder needs and on supporting the operations of the campus by facilitating communication and cooperation among offices and programs.

Methods used to build communication and promote cohesiveness among campus employees include a faculty and staff fall retreat, monthly birthday celebrations, faculty and staff luncheons and meetings, monthly publication of Campus Connection, the library Media Mania publication, ethics training, leadership labs, and the annual recognition and awards banquet. To improve campus-wide communication, the college now posts the minutes of all committee meetings on the college web site and uses email to keep the campus community informed and to provide the opportunity for faculty and staff feedback.

Its work systems design enables NMSU–C to keep current with educational service and student development needs through several channels: departmental needs-response initiatives, inter-departmental collaboration and planning, ongoing student and stakeholder needs assessment, external/internal program review processes, and peer college comparison.

Leadership provides a number of opportunities each year to foster collaboration, innovation, and individual initiative. Motivation of faculty and staff begins with regular opportunities for personal and professional development. For example, all faculty and staff are encouraged to enroll in free classes, to attend local, regional, and state conferences, to participate in college-sponsored training sessions, and to assume leadership roles on college governance and planning committees.

NMSU–C's small size and active campus community participation in all key processes facilitate superior communication, cooperation, and knowledge sharing across areas. The campus committee developed a mentoring process, which was implemented in fall 2002, and which ensures the smooth transition of new employees into their positions and the campus community. Employee satisfaction with work systems, work design, and the overall campus environment is evidenced in the results of the nationally recognized PACE (Personal Assessment of Campus Environment) survey.

Performance Management

The college's goals are stakeholder satisfaction, high performance, and student learning. The management system supports the improvement of individual and institutional performance through the following means: annual evaluations of all faculty, administration, and classified staff, and those receiving "satisfactory" evaluations are awarded increases in compensation; employee recognition systems and ceremonies at both the department and college levels; regular departmental meetings, which provide an occasion for ongoing feedback and recognition of employee efforts; annual meetings between supervisors and employees to discuss goals and objectives for the coming year; and daily meetings and work sessions during which supervisors discuss progress toward goals and objectives.

Leadership Development

Historically, qualified senior leaders at NMSU–C are recruited from outside the institution. NMSU–C's size eliminates the need for numerous second and third tier administrators (vice presidents, deans); therefore, most top-level administrative duties differ substantially from the normal duties of faculty and staff and require different educational preparation. The duties of senior leaders also differ substantially from one another, both in academic preparation and experience. NMSU–C relies on pools of qualified applicants whose administrative experience has been earned at other institutions. This system allows the college to benefit from the best practices of a diverse range of academic institutions.

One exception to this general rule is the position of division coordinator, which combines faculty and administrative duties and provides enough administrative experience that talented division coordinators are encouraged to apply for senior leadership positions. NMSU–Las Cruces recently made available to branch campuses a new program offering graduate degrees in community college leadership. NMSU–C pays the tuition of current employees who enroll in the program. Graduates of this program will be qualified to fill senior leadership positions.

Training, Education, and Development

Faculty and staff development and personal growth are integral to the culture of the college, evidenced by the fact that they are directly supported by key action plans and school needs. Campus-wide participation fosters the development of ideas and opportunities for improvement of the college culture. These aspects of the campus ensure that the workforce is continuously trained, multi-skilled, and empowered.

NMSU–C designs action plans to meet school needs. Major action plans include faculty and staff professional development, continuing accreditation, outreach, student assessment and achievement, and technology literacy. NMSU–C realizes the need for development of faculty and staff; therefore, commitment to faculty and staff development and personal growth is an integral part of the culture of the college environment. The college provides time and resources for education, training, and personal/professional development and expects faculty and staff to apply their increased educational and technological expertise in the classroom and/or work area. Several examples of education and training that meet these needs are attendance by campus representatives at the North Central Association's annual meeting and at a statewide assessment conference, developing and providing a course for faculty for instructing via ITV, and a campus-wide workshop on developmental education.

The campus executive leadership primarily facilitates education training and design. Classified staff, professional staff, and faculty provide input into training and design through several means. For example, classified staff contribute through survey responses and monthly meetings. Full-time faculty receive financial support to attend conferences and workshops that foster professional development. All faculty members have schedule flexibility to pursue advanced academic study. Tuition is paid for faculty and staff members seeking advanced degrees through the on-campus NMSU offerings in higher education leadership.

Classified staff, professional staff, and faculty (full-time and part-time) training and development are accomplished through classes and seminars conducted on site or by attendance at national, regional, or local workshops. Examples of on-campus offerings include an Americans with Disabilities Act issues workshop, budget and purchasing workshops, communication and sensitivity workshops, a grant-writing workshop, software training, course management system training, and Quality New Mexico examiner training.

Participants evaluate all education and training activities through questionnaires. Campus leadership recognizes that the quality of school performance depends upon staff and faculty skill, motivation, and performance. To that end, training and education opportunities for faculty and staff are carefully formulated. Annual performance evaluations recognize and reward the training and education completed during the evaluation year as well as the completion of set goals and the development of future goals.

An example of reinforcing skills gained to improve organizational performance is technical training. During annual employee evaluation cycles, campus leaders identify goals for technical development of employees, including learning such skills as web site creation and management, database applications, and technical presentation training. Evaluation results provide data that are utilized in planning internal and external training for technical competency areas. When training is completed, employees reinforce their new and improved skills by using them in the workplace, and their performance is evaluated in the next evaluation cycle.

Faculty and Staff Satisfaction

NMSU–C relies on a variety of mechanisms to measure faculty and staff satisfaction and institutional success. Faculty and staff rate the campus climate and environment using the PACE survey, a nationally administered instrument developed by the National Initiative for Leadership and Institutional Effectiveness. This survey provides each employee the opportunity to assess the campus using the categories of formal influence, communication, collaboration, organizational structure, work design, technology, student focus, and overall climate.

The PACE survey has been administered three times since 1998 and the results shared with all constituencies. Results demonstrate that employees perceive the institutional climate to be highly consultative and collaborative and that institutional leaders adhere to the core values of valuing employees and partnership development. Nevertheless, one result of the PACE that resulted in a priority for improvement was NMSU–C's score on communications. Though it was higher than the national average, the communication score was the lowest of all of NMSU–C's measures, so the campus identified and instituted several methods of improving communications, including town hall meetings and a monthly newsletter.

Administering the Campus Quality Survey (CQS) is a new addition to the campus processes. Both PACE and CQS are anonymous and provide opportunities for employees to voice concerns. The specific results and conclusions derived from PACE and CQS provide the foundation for developing improvement priorities for campus operations and leadership.

As these priorities are addressed, improvements in results are tracked in subsequent years.

Employee retention is high and absenteeism is low. No grievances have been filed since 1995. Another measure of employee morale is level of participation in campus activities. For example, 34% of full-time employees participated in workshops focused on quality-based methods in higher education, completing Quality New Mexico examiner training. Employees may take one course per semester free of charge, and nine members of the campus community are enrolled in or have graduated from the NMSU graduate degree program in community college leadership. Numerous methods are used to recognize and reward faculty and staff (see Figure 4.6).

Process Management

NMSU–C delivers high-quality academic and nonacademic programs. Academic programs are designed to maximize student success and meet stakeholder needs. A wide range of input sources and resources are integral to the campus planning and implementation processes.

Program Design

NMSU–C's design process is an integral part of its planning process. The college offers certificate programs and courses at the freshman and sophomore levels, and has the flexibility to design and implement associate degrees, certificates, credit courses, and customized training to meet identified stakeholder needs. Faculty, in consultation with the appropriate advisory committee and other interested stakeholders, design and implement associate degrees, certificates, and courses in direct response to needs voiced by local stakeholders. For example, NMSU–C designed and implemented a heritage interpretation associate degree, a process that involved NMSU–C campus leadership, the NMSU Faculty Senate, the dean of the College of Health and Social Services, the faculty of the history department at NMSU, and the NMSU Board of Regents. New programs and new course designs are implemented and approved as part of the strategy development process.

Manufacturing sector development course and program offerings are also directly responsive to the community, determined by needs voiced by

Figure 4.6

Methods of Recognizing and Rewarding Faculty and Staff at
New Mexico State University–Carlsbad

Formal Methods	Informal Methods
• Annual evaluations—all employees • Recognition ceremony (employee appreciation) • Service awards (certificates and/or gifts) • Free classes (all regular employees, one course per semester)	• In-house birthday celebrations • Employee praise/recognition by supervisor • Departmental dinners/lunches for employees • Flexible work hours
• Sponsored professional development opportunities (workshops, seminars) • Tuition reduction policy/practice • Release time for training, teaching, recruitment, special projects, and advanced degree work • Salary increase for advanced degree completion • Incentive pay increase for increased productivity, promotions, and longevity • Participation by all employee groups on committees • Generous annual leave, sick leave, and holiday leave time allowances/policies • NISOD Excellence Award	• Compensation for overtime • Departmental and employee publicity • Safe, friendly work environment • Employee cross training • Opportunities to experiment • Committee feedback to initiatives • Inclusion of all employee names/positions in campus publications • Opportunities to develop new initiatives

local businesses, industries, and government social service agencies. These offerings may be as focused as the development and implementation of an apprenticeship program for the construction trades. To create such a program, the Manufacturing Sector Development program follows the established best-practice methods of similar programs in the region and nation.

Academic programs are managed through a process that includes leadership oversight and program review, which centers on strengthening curricula and programs through assessing enrollment patterns, reviewing retention rates, assessing academic standards, and reviewing graduate placement and success rates for program-specific certifications.

The chief academic officer delegates the responsibility for developing academic course schedules and distributing teaching loads to the division coordinators, whose decisions are made in consultation with full-time faculty. The aim of the scheduling process is to maximize student success rates and to increase the average course enrollments by meeting stakeholder needs. Trend and needs analyses, based on data from course history (enrollment figures for each course for the previous six years), and placement testing drive the course scheduling process. These data and new enrollment estimates allow academic leadership to make informed decisions about course offerings. The key performance measures of courses and programs include elements such as course success rates, campus retention rates, cohort success rates, program specific successes, and graduate placement data.

Associate degrees offered by NMSU–C require a core of general education courses, including credits in English, mathematics, critical thinking skills, history, the natural sciences, human thought and behavior, social analysis, information retrieval, and literature and fine arts. These general education courses are offered every semester to meet student academic progression needs. All NMSU–C credit courses use a standardized syllabus format that provides a description in each syllabus of the course-specific methods for evaluating student learning and the nine graduate outcomes associated with each specific course. Students integrate outcome assessments into the process within the course evaluations. Multiple sections of the same course have standardized final exams to ensure consistency of learning and skills.

The campus uses a wide array of observations, measures, and indicators to assess student learning and ensure quality and consistency of educational programs (see Figure 4.7). The campus-based program review process regularly evaluates programs. This analysis leads to recommendations for improvement of course content and program efficiency. Student

Figure 4.7

Formative and Summative Assessment Methods at New Mexico State University–Carlsbad

Formative Measures	Summative Measures
Portfolios	Course exit assessments
Midterm exams	Advanced placement exam
Quizzes	Credit by exam
Papers and/or projects	Final exams
Oral presentations	Licensure exams
Internships	Employer feedback

success is also measured and evaluated as a segment of this process. Program review results are shared through the campus governance structure.

Support Processes

The school designs its support processes to encourage a learning-centered environment. NMSU–C's strategy development process leads to the improvement of support processes and the implementation of new processes. NMSU–C's key educational support processes have been operating for many years, have been refined, and continue to be improved, through use, as part of the continuous quality-improvement process. The review of measures, such as utilization statistics and satisfaction levels, is integral to the continuous improvement of these processes.

Key educational support processes and their respective requirements, measures, management, in-process measures, evaluation, and process improvement that achieve better performance have been clearly identified by the campus. One example of campus support of key educational support processes is the student services' Student Success Model, which includes all services and support provided by staff and faculty as well as the flow of students through the institution to ensure proper placement in classes and eventual academic success. Key educational support processes are periodically reviewed for accuracy and reliability. Inputs into and feedback from these processes are integrated into the NMSU–C planning process.

Feedback on the services provided by student services is collected from the Student Opinion Survey, which is administered each spring semester. Each service component tracks the number of students who use the services, and key areas such as financial aid, tutoring, and orientations have created their own internal satisfaction surveys. The coordinators of the areas use survey results to adjust, adapt, and improve processes. Feedback is also received from the Student Interests Committee. This committee, composed of faculty, students, and staff, annually reviews the survey results and serves as a focus group that advises student services of emerging needs.

NMSU–C provides a broad array of support services, including financial aid, advising, tutoring, special needs coordination and referrals to outside agencies for social problems beyond the scope of campus capacity. Each component of student services audits its services using the standards and guidelines developed by the Council for the Advancement of Standards in Higher Education. Aligning with national standards ensures that local student services meet or exceed a national baseline of service. These standards and guidelines provide information about delivery methods used at comparable institutions.

The campus also uses input from the Adult Learners Needs Survey (ALNS) so that services can be adjusted to meet students' needs. The ALNS is administered every three years and then reviewed by staff. Action plans are developed to address the prominent needs the survey identifies. The Student Opinion Survey drives action plans in years one and two, and the satisfaction levels of students are closely monitored. In year three, the ALNS is administered again, and another list of priorities is developed from student input. The cycle is continuous, with action plans developed and services modified and/or implemented according to survey results.

The day-to-day operation of support processes is the responsibility of the managers of each area, who meet with staff regularly or as needed. Weekly meetings of the campus executive officers ensure that progress toward meeting key performance requirements is tracked and analyzed. Regular meetings of the division coordinators provide opportunities for all college managers to discuss college-wide issues and to interact formally with senior leaders.

Key performance and satisfaction measures are evaluated annually. In addition, most areas conduct periodic surveys to assess satisfaction with services and then make adjustments.

5

National University

Patricia E. Potter, A. Cathleen Greiner

National University (NU) is the second largest private, nonprofit institution of higher education in California. It was founded in 1971 and is regionally accredited by the Western Association of Schools and Colleges. NU has 28 locations throughout California and a 722-mile footprint that reaches from its Chula Vista campus to Redding. The university offers degrees at the associate, bachelor's, and master's levels, serving more than 17,000 students each year. Courses are taught in the classroom and via the Internet. NU also brings its educational programs to students throughout corporate worksites, police and sheriffs' academies, border patrol offices, hospitals, military bases, government facilities, and schools. The university's mission is a simple one: "To make lifelong learning opportunities accessible, challenging and relevant to a diverse population of adult learners." Its six core values are quality, access, relevance, accelerated pace, affordability, and community.

National University's Culture of Quality

National University (NU) has been committed to serving the needs of adult learners since its beginning, and the institution's story is one of a renegade in American higher education. Its culture of quality was formed by three key events: 1) its founding as a nontraditional institution of higher education, 2) the economic depression the university suffered in the late 1980s, and 3) the commitment of its second president to the development of quality systems that would allow the institution to develop its quality culture.

The notion that a university with access as a core value could provide rigorous academic programs to adult students in an accelerated format was an affront to the higher education establishment in the 1970s. Standardized test scores and high school rankings were often the only acceptable measures of student "quality." The traditional message to students was clear—higher education for adults was reserved for those who were able to bend their lives to the institution's format and calendar. In 1971, NU was established to serve adult learners through evening programs offered in a course per month format. The university didn't necessarily set out to be different; it set out to be relevant.

The second event that shaped NU's culture of quality was its near collapse in 1988. Seventeen years after its founding, in the waning days of the tenure of its first and founding president, NU entered a period of severe financial and accreditation challenges. The university was on the brink of economic and academic collapse—more than $10 million in debt, no endowment, and shrinking enrollments. This profound experience creates an indelible change in an institution's culture.

The third dominating influence on NU's culture is its second and current president, Jerry C. Lee. He infused the struggling institution with an entrepreneurial can-do spirit and engendered among the faculty and staff a commitment to an articulated mission and a set of core values. Total Quality Management (TQM), which was instituted in 1990, helped bring the university back to a solid financial footing and left a cultural legacy that is visible in the institution's willingness to embrace rapid change, innovation, and accountability.

Beginning the Quality Journey

By 1992, the university's accreditation was reaffirmed by the Western Association of Schools and Colleges. As the institution regained financial health, it chose to commit substantial resources and effort to the fortification of its academic soundness. Early efforts at institutional quality improvement occurred between 1992 and 1995. TQM initiatives were implemented university-wide to improve operating efficiencies and guarantee quality standards in academic programs. In 1993, uniform administrative structures were implemented to balance administrative functions university wide.

In September 1994, "A Vision for Academic Year 2000" first articulated NU's desire to become the premier institution for adult learners. The following year, the institution completed its first five-year strategic plan. In August 1996, a discussion paper titled "National University: An Environment of Quality" outlined a plan that called for a "conscious and consistent effort to establish a culture of quality at National University" (Lee, 1996). The challenge, of course, was to identify the specific actions that would be required to achieve this desired culture.

In 1997, NU took the first step to implement a model of institutional effectiveness. The components of this institution-wide model for continuous improvement included the development of purpose statements and objectives in each operating unit to support the institution's mission and goals; the collection, analysis, and use of data to assess whether the objectives were met; and evidence of improvement-based assessment (Nichols, 1995).

As a tuition-dependent, private institution, NU did not have several years to implement this new model of effectiveness. To encourage accelerated acceptance of the model, every operating unit was required to report to key members of the university community on the outcomes of the assessment processes at an assessment summit. The first assessment summit was held in September 1998 and the summits have continued on an annual basis, helping to maintain the institution's focus on continuous improvement.

Adopting the Baldrige Criteria

In 1997, presidential commissions were appointed to study and report on aspects of the institution's operations that required improvement. Each commission was composed of a broad cross section of faculty, staff, and administrators from all areas of the university. In 2000, the Commission on Academic Rigor and Quality was formed, and its final report contained 48 recommendations to enhance quality in all academic areas. Much of the report referred to the Baldrige education criteria for performance excellence and recommended that quality be adopted as the university's sixth core value. In 2001, the university committed to pursue the Malcolm Baldrige National Quality Award.

In 2002, the institution submitted its first Baldrige application, as well as an application for the California Council on Excellence awards program, and was named the recipient of a third-place bronze Eureka Award at the state level. In 2003, the university once again prepared Baldrige and state applications. Although the institution has yet to be recognized by the Baldrige program, the California Council for Excellence did select NU for a site visit, and the institution received a second Eureka Award.

More importantly, the institution received two very comprehensive feedback reports that outlined numerous opportunities for improvement. These documents provided a cornerstone to reshape the institution's approach to the Baldrige process and to accreditation. In 2004, the university decided not to submit further applications at the state and national level and to spend at least 18 months working on the implementation of the suggestions for improvement. NU's quality journey, spanning more than three decades, is summarized in Figure 5.1.

Organizational Leadership

Consistency is a hallmark of quality, and NU has benefited from the consistent commitment and steady focus of its president. According to the American Council on Education (2002), the average length of service as president was 6.6 years in 2001. The current president of NU has served the institution for more than 15 years. Because of this exceptionally long tenure, the university has been able to avoid the turmoil and the distractions that inevitably accompany changes in leadership. It has also been spared from changes in institutional direction.

The senior leadership team—the president, provost, and vice presidents—develop directions and objectives and share them with the deans, directors, department chairs, faculty, managers, and other staff to ensure that short- and longer-term directions cascade down through the organization in an aligned fashion. The mission and values are the basis for setting strategic directions, prioritizing budget requests, setting department and individual objectives, and chartering presidential commissions on critical

Figure 5.1
The Quality Journey at National University

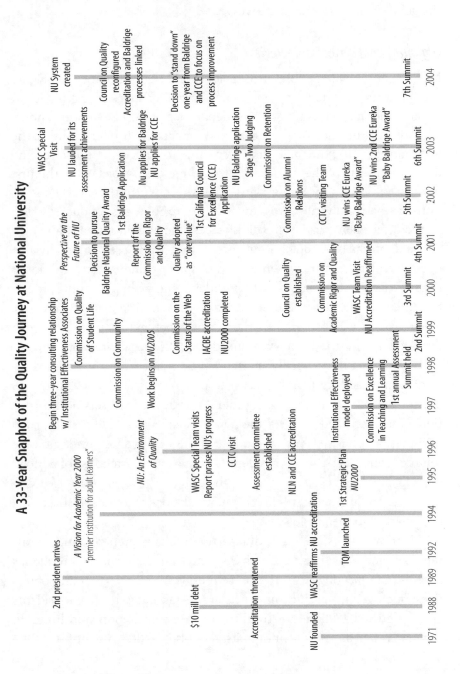

A 33-Year Snapshot of the Quality Journey at National University

issues. Individual performance expectations are tied to these directions, and individual performance is evaluated at midterm and year end against the achievement of these objectives.

Organizational Performance Review

NU's organizational performance review cycle begins in June (see Figure 5.2), and the president announces any formal changes to the organizational structure at this time. Thus, department heads have prior knowledge of institutional changes that may impact their operations in the upcoming year. At the same time, departments review the successes and disappointments of the prior year. From these discussions come the first outlines of division operating plans. The way in which these early discussions are managed varies across the institution. Some are conducted solely by the department head, some divisions engage in mini-retreats, and others hold informal roundtables. July is spent preparing preliminary division operation plans that are presented at the August planning retreat. Prior to the retreat, the president and vice presidents engage in a planning process that links the agenda to the mission and the strategic planning process. The retreat provides a forum for the review of preliminary plans from each division and how those plans are linked to the strategic direction.

The annual fall assembly is attended by members of the administration, faculty, and staff, and webcast to employees outside of San Diego. The president, incorporating the themes of the retreat, sets out institutional directions and goals for the new academic year. Additionally, each vice president has separate meetings with his or her division to reinforce the president's message. A presidential commission, composed of a broad group of faculty and staff from across the university, is established to investigate, report, and make specific recommendations on critical institutional issues linked to the mission.

Next, managers, deans, and department chairs prepare annual written goals and objectives in response to the strategic plan, the president's address, and meetings with their vice presidents. Those goals and objectives, anchored in specific outcomes, are reviewed by the vice presidents and form the backbone for the Program Annual Report and Program Review, as well as assessment of units, schools, and departments.

Figure 5.2

The Organizational Performance Review Cycle at National University

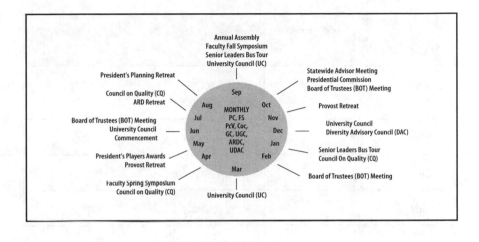

In the spring and fall, full-time and associate faculty gather for a faculty symposium where they discuss effective learning and teaching, and communicate concerns to deans and department chairs, who in turn advise senior leaders. The assessment summit in the fall brings the university community together for a formal report of departmental progress on goals and objectives. The summit provides another opportunity to assess progress and, if necessary, correct course or chart a new one. The midyear performance review process in January and final performance reviews in June bring the assessment process to the individual level. In 2000, the Council on Quality was established to complement the focus on the Baldrige criteria. This forum is devoted to assessing institutional progress toward meeting the criteria.

NU's key performance measures are shown in Figure 5.3. These represent only the dashboard indicators. Reports are provided weekly, monthly, quarterly, and annually, or on an as needed basis, to senior leaders via the Executive Query System. Senior leaders also compare performance against other institutions in the state and nationally when comparative data and benchmarks are available. Relevant indicators are reviewed by campus location and by the senior leadership at each center.

Figure 5.3
Key Performance Measures at National University

Linked to Core Value	Indicator	Measure	Frequency
Quality	AI	Student course evaluation date	Monthly
Quality	AI	Grade point average	Monthly
Quality	AI	Average class size	Monthly
Quality	AI	Active students	Monthly
Quality	AI	Faculty with terminal degrees	Quarterly
Access	AI	Persistence, retention, and graduation	Quarterly
Access	AI	Enrollments by program, location	Weekly
Access	AI	Minority enrollments	Quarterly
Affordability	AI	Growth in endowment	Monthly
Relevance	AI	Program review cycle	Annually
Quality	FI	Prager ratios	Annually
Access	FI	New admissions	Weekly
Access	FI	Students in class	Weekly
Affordability	FI	Days tuition outstanding	Monthly

Linked to Core Value	Indicator	Measure	Frequency
Affordability	FI	Financial aid cohort default rate	Monthly
Quality	SI	Safety reports	Monthly
Access	SI	Matriculation rates	Quarterly
Relevance	SI	Growth in online alumni community	Monthly
Affordability	SI	Comparative tuition data	Annually
Accelerated Pace	SI	Network health indicators	Hourly
Accelerated Pace	SI	Advisor development reports	Monthly
Community	SI	Statewide media reports	Monthly
Community	SI	Media and markets report	Monthly
AI = Academic Indicator	**FI = Fiscal Indicator**		**SI = Service Indicator**

Senior leaders review academic performance and improvement—the focus toward which all performance reviews must contribute. They review data on performance in several areas:

- Courses, programs, departments, and schools through the use of program reviews, accreditation reports, external evaluations, and benchmarking studies
- Faculty and deans through midyear and end-of-year progress on goals, monthly student evaluations of instruction, and applications for reappointment, merit, and promotion

- Students through placement test results for English and math skills at matriculation, GPA, progress toward degrees, capstone course completions, and results on exams

Strategic Planning Processes

Of the core activities undertaken by any institution, strategic planning is among the most essential. It is crucial in aligning institutional values, actions, aspirations, and everyday operations and functions. For NU, strategic planning is both an essential process and an environmental document that informs annual budgets, priorities, and activities, and serves as the overarching connection to organizational goals and objectives.

The institution has created two strategic plans (NU 2000, NU 2005) and is in the initial phase of a third (NU 2010). As a systematic quality initiative, the strategic planning process is firmly built on understanding what has occurred and reflecting on accomplishments—deriving meaning from lessons learned to create a new baseline for the future.

Strategic planning provides vision and direction for NU's long-range efforts to meet its mission. Operational planning provides for implementation of the strategic planning framework in the day-to-day environment. The annual planning process, resource allocation, and budgetary process, as well as assessment of accomplishment, are derived from and linked to the current plan, NU 2005 (see Figure 5.4).

Several steps were involved in developing NU 2005, including an evaluation of accomplishments of NU 2000, the official initiation of a new planning process, and the authorization of a planning group to develop a detailed timeline with deliverable action items. An important step in developing the current plan was the broad participation of the NU community; such inclusiveness is considered a best practice for strategic planning. For example, in developing NU 2005, input was obtained from the board of trustees, faculty, administration, staff, and students statewide. This consultative process ensured systemic involvement and clear understanding of the direction and goals of the planning outcome. Extensive dialogue with external consultants and experts provided an objective viewpoint and professional analysis.

The strategic plan is a contextual structure dedicated to the institution's vision. Operational plans then form the annual, or short-term, components used to achieve progress. The annual planning process builds on

Figure 5.4
Strategic Plan Development at National University

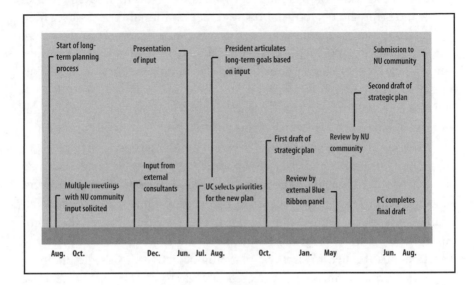

the strategic plan by delineating the tactics that the academic and administrative units implement within the context of the day-to-day environment. By design, the strategic objectives serve as the supporting and coordinating framework of university-wide planning activities and are derived from the strategic directions or goals. Assessment of the effectiveness of units and departments in meeting the objectives of the operational plans provides the data for determining progress in meeting strategic objectives. This is a built-in feedback loop that allows the institution to identify directions requiring additional emphasis.

The most relevant characteristic of the strategic planning process at NU is its flexibility. While the need for a long-term perspective is clearly recognized, the objectives and timelines are not set in stone. Through continuous assessment of achievement of shared goals, new goals may be added as a result of successful accomplishment (e.g., completing the state-of-the-art library building) or when external circumstances require a shift in the long-term focus (e.g., adding allied entities to expand the university's base of operations). The strategic directions are clearly communicated to the board of trustees, senior leaders, faculty, and staff.

NU 2005 is a master document that contains goals and objectives that are quantifiable and aspirational. The university ensures that strategic planning addresses core themes and values by assessing strategic directions and strategic objectives in a systematic, annual process by which operational and academic units gather evidence, interpret and analyze the information, implement change, and identify outcomes and actions that indicate change over time. Tracking each objective annually reveals incremental changes that contribute to noted advances. Changes in each objective are analyzed in three areas: description, evidence, and validation (internal or external). Using this process, NU continually emphasizes the question: "How do we know?"

An important component of the planning process is linking the annual budget to the university's strategic planning directions and objections. The annual budget process occurs in two phases. Phase one is the development of baseline budgets at the department level to ensure the ongoing funding of initiatives. All requests for additional dollars beyond the baseline must be tied to strategic planning objectives. Strategic planning objective requests must be connected directly to the strategic directives and objectives in NU 2005.

Phase two of the process begins when all baseline and Special Planning Objective budget requests must be reviewed and approved by the budget unit head before such requests are forwarded to the university budget committee, which is composed of the provost and the vice presidents. This committee reaches consensus on budget priorities for Special Planning Objectives by answering the following two questions: 1) To what degree does the requested Special Planning Objective promote the long-term objectives outlined in NU 2005 and academic quality? 2) Does the requested Special Planning Objective address other issues that have become relevant since these long-term plans were finalized? The budgeting process provides administrative and academic entities enough freedom to translate these goals to meet the current and changing realities that impact the institution or could not be foreseen at the time the documents were developed. The process also promotes flexibility to respond to program opportunities or economic concerns.

NU's short- and long-term action plans are embedded in its eight distinct plans, including NU 2005, the five-year strategic plan, Academic Agenda, Technology Plan, Diversity Plan, Facilities Plan, Budget Plan,

Marketing and Enrollment Plan, and Student Services Plan. Since 1998, key changes in the university's service and programs, driven from one or more of the various plans, include increasing the number of online courses/ programs, implementing web-based student grade reporting, upgrading classroom facilities in 13 locations, constructing 475,600 new square feet of academic facilities, establishing the largest e-book collection in a non-system academic library in the United States, and implementing an online community for alumni.

A new activity related to aligning strategic planning and institutional improvement and assessing systematic processes to accomplish this is the university's participation in the Malcolm Baldrige National Quality Award process. The first submission provided useful feedback, including emphasis on reviewing processes and linking strategic goals and planning activities. The nature of the Baldrige application structure is such that the university was required to develop an articulated analysis and understanding of itself and its operations, with extensive reference to analyzed and interpreted quantitative and qualitative data in the context of various benchmarks and targets relevant to the institution's mission, values, and operations.

By remaining flexible and adhering to an annual assessment structure and data-centric perspective, strategic decisions are strengthened. In this way, NU focuses on the process by which objectives and learning goals are determined; appropriate measures are selected; data collection, analysis, and distribution are organized; and decisions are made. The university's environment is reflective in that it uses analysis and evidence to understand the past and inform the future. It is the NU community's responsibility to ask the right questions and to seek appropriate data and measures to guide the institution in reaching its strategic goals.

Student and Stakeholder Focus

NU's student market segment has been clearly defined as the adult learner. Admission typically requires that students have work experience (normally five years). The average age of graduate students, who comprise 70% of the total enrollment, is 34. The average age of the undergraduate population is 33. NU serves as the primary, independent transfer institution for students from community colleges. To facilitate transfer, NU has developed formalized articulation agreements addressing the general education curriculum and the professional curriculum.

As the leader in the preparation of California teachers, NU has student teaching contracts with 643 districts in 50 counties, more than any other institution in the state. NU recommends more candidates for their preliminary teaching credentials than any other single institution of higher education in California. Since 1971, NU has been a primary provider of graduate and undergraduate education to military personnel and currently provides classrooms and instruction on six military installations in southern California.

Listening to Student Needs

NU monitors and assesses student expectations and attitudes from the point of initial contact through graduation and into students' professional careers. It utilizes several internal and external listening and learning approaches to identify needs and to establish and improve a supportive student environment (see Figure 5.5).

Prior to admission, a prospective student is interviewed by an advisor who provides an overview of NU's format and program offerings and ascertains the student's educational needs and career aspirations to determine if the person is a good candidate for the university's unique climate and structure. The advisor offers guidance about the admission process and transferability of previous coursework; orients the student to program-specific requirements, support services, and procedures; and assists with initial scheduling of courses.

A faculty advisor is identified to assist the student throughout the program. Specialized support units exist to meet the needs of disabled, international, remedial, military, and credential students. All incoming undergraduate students who have not met their basic college-level math or English requirements are required to take placement tests to determine the strength of their skills so that students with deficiencies can enhance their opportunity for success through specialized coursework and tutoring.

Students are segmented by academic program. Given that over 58% of post-baccalaureate students are in credential programs, NU provides them with an additional set of designated advisors—credential advisors—to guide them through the credentialing process. Certain programs, like those for teacher credentialing and counseling psychology, have special-

Figure 5.5

Primary Student Feedback Sources at National University

Student Listening and Learning Method	Student Group
Intake interviews	Prospective
Adult learner needs assessment	New
Accuplacer test	New
Orientations	New
Staff liaisons for departments	Current
Course evaluations	Current
Student complaints	Current
Student services survey	Current
Exit interviews	Former
Teacher forums/surveys	Alumni
Alumni survey/gatherings	Alumni

ized, individual, or group orientations to provide academic advisement and information regarding professional licensure. Each academic program has a designated lead faculty member with whom students may interact to gain further information or to offer constructive feedback. Every month students evaluate each course, its instruction, and the instructor. Results are forwarded to department chairs and deans and to the Office of Academic Affairs.

Programs annually engage in learning-outcome assessment and evaluation of student and faculty profiles. Every five years, faculty undertake a comprehensive review to ensure that programs are meeting student and stakeholder needs and expectations. Educational improvements are also assessed annually against initiatives in NU 2005. Current students, alumni, employers, and other stakeholders are surveyed to determine satisfaction with the university's services, programs, and products.

In keeping with NU's core value of relevance, surveys conducted since 2000 have revealed that student satisfaction with the application of NU's degree programs to real-world needs has been consistent at 88% or higher. This figure is significant because the student population consists of working professionals with firsthand knowledge of the demands of their professions. Moreover, findings and comments on the alumni survey indicate that graduates are pleased with their level of academic preparation for their chosen fields. Since 1998, the results of the Master Teacher Survey indicate a satisfaction rate of 98% among school personnel with the preparation of teacher candidates.

Individual divisions initiate surveys specific to their areas. In 1998, for example, 587 business majors were surveyed about their interest in online programs, their level of Internet access, and interest in a two-month format. This information formed the basis for NU's development of online degree programs and the two-month, online courses for the Executive MBA program. These programs have been extremely successful; enrollments in online courses have grown from 175 students in 2001 to more than 3,000 in 2004.

Information from the annual satisfaction survey, which has been administered since 1994, is used routinely to enhance, improve, or introduce new services that will better meet student needs (see Figure 5.6). NU's internal benchmark for satisfaction levels with student services is 80%. Each year, survey results are reviewed by all vice presidents and department managers whose units are responsible for student services. Regional managers also review the survey results and develop action plans to address areas that are below the benchmark.

Improving Student Learning and Performance

Regional accreditation of higher education institutions is an important part of accomplishing several goals, including a broad-based assurance of quality, ease of transferability of credits, access to federal funds, and a substantiation of product reliability for employers. The typical review involves reflective self-study, peer review, site visits, and recommendations regard-

Figure 5.6

Alumni Survey Results at National University

National University Alumni Survey	2000	2002	Increase
Extent to which NU degree is valuable.	95	96	1%
	Strongly Agree/Agree		
Did NU degree help attain current workplace position or status?	79	80	1%
	Very/Somewhat helpful		
How helpful was NU degree for job possessed at time of leaving NU?	63	80	17%
	Very/Somewhat helpful		
How satisfied were you with quality of academic program at NU?	87	92	5%
	Very/Somewhat helpful		
Would you choose NU to pursue another degree?	69	73	4%
	Yes/Probably		

ing areas of focus for institutional improvement. The embedded outcome is ongoing attention to the process of persistently pursuing progress in regard to quality and the product of the educational enterprise—learners who can combine and use theory and application.

NU consistently devotes time and attention to the accrediting process. The outcomes provide a blueprint for detailed institutional focus on key areas. The most recent visit by the institution's accreditation team provides a case in point and details the university's emphasis on improving quality. Focusing on the institution's mission, strategic planning cycles, and annual attention to goals provides a framework to respond to opportunities and improve academic and service abilities.

The current phase of NU's history is characterized by dedicated attention to academic quality along with the historic focus on access, internal and external assessment and response to change, and planning for new initiatives. Some activities associated with quality included inviting external professional groups and panels of experts to review multiple aspects of the university's work and responding to their recommendations, initiation of the use of academic indicators to enhance faculty effectiveness and program quality, and implementation of a systematic process of assessment and analysis of student learning outcomes. By following its usual pattern of using previous accreditation visits to prepare for the upcoming cycle, NU used findings and key points to develop themes in planning for a visit in spring 2003:

- Clarified the educational and strategic goals of the institution

- Improved its assessment activities to determine, analyze, and report progress within the context of the themes

- Implemented actions judged to be appropriate responses to the results of assessment activities

This theme—academic rigor and quality—focused on three sets of issues the university developed in response to the accreditation findings: the one-month format, grade inflation, and student retention.

Instructional Delivery Strategies: One-Month Format

A one-month intensive study format was initiated at NU. Instead of taking three to four courses over a four-month semester, students focus on one subject at a time. This format often challenges academics and institutions of higher education that are accustomed to more traditional schedules. Nevertheless, the university has concluded that this type of schedule—increasingly employed by institutions that focus on adult learners—is effective. The university's annual alumni survey provides consistent evidence of student satisfaction with NU's academic program and applicability to the workplace.

In addition to multiple annual student surveys, the university has conducted several research studies to review the effectiveness of the compressed course format (Schwartz, 2002; Serdyukov, Subbotin, & Serdyukova, 2002; Tatum & Parker, 2002). These studies led to three key findings: 1) there were no significant differences in learning outcomes between the two formats, 2) students in the three-month format felt that they had more time to complete outside assignments, and 3) students in the one-month format were more satisfied and more willing to recommend the format to their peers. These efforts indicate a specific emphasis on studying and critiquing the effectiveness of accelerated learning and the intensive format.

Addressing Grade Inflation

Since the mid-1960s, grade inflation has been a tough issue for universities to understand and address. With support from all academic areas of the university, NU decided to address this issue directly. The basic approach has been to focus on the academic rigor and quality of course content and requirements, on the assumption that as rigor and quality increase, there will be a concomitant shift in the distribution of student grades.

With this strategy in mind, the university established target mean GPAs at 2.75 for undergraduate programs and 3.25 for graduate programs. Training on scoring and grading was implemented; and deans and chairs discussed with faculty members the plan to reduce the average GPA. One consideration was that the student body (typical age in the mid-30s) is, on average, more serious and more motivated than a traditional undergraduate student body. It is not surprising that adult learners perform at higher levels. Several studies demonstrate that nontraditional students have greater motivation and personal management skills and that their GPAs are higher than those of traditional students (Spitzer, 2000; Zemke & Zemke, 1984).

With a goal and plan in place, the process moved forward over a two-year time period and yielded good results. The encouraging success of NU's initiative to reduce grade inflation by improving academic rigor and quality is apparent in a review of the multiyear mean grade data in the following charts, which analyze mean grades earned over time by educational level across the institution (see Figure 5.7).

The analysis revealed a consistent downward trend in the level of GPAs across schools and the university. Further analysis was done on the number of "A" grades awarded. Between 1998 and 2002, the percentage

Figure 5.7

Mean Grades Earned Over Time at National University

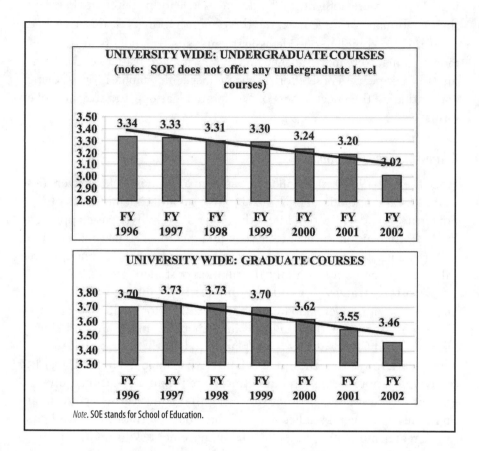

Note. SOE stands for School of Education.

of "A's" awarded for students in associate degree programs declined nearly 8%. Among bachelor's degree students, the decline was 10%, and for master's degree and credential students the percentage of "A's" awarded declined 4%. The largest change in the dispersion of "A's" is indicated from 2000 to 2002 when the university increased its emphasis on GPAs (see Figure 5.8).

One important tool in addressing the relationship between academic rigor and grade inflation has been the development of a report that provides the mean grade data for each class taught at the university. The report provides summary data for the institution, but also supports closer

Figure 5.8

Annual Changes in Percentage of "A's" Awarded at National University

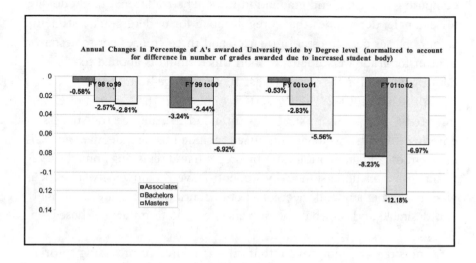

examination of mean class grades in a variety of configurations, such as, average GPAs for classes with fewer than 10 students versus larger classes. Although the main report is organized around schools, departments, and locations, it is also possible to look at average GPAs by program. In short, the report helps NU take action as necessary, such as identifying classes and instructors with consistently and improbably high average grades, and classes and instructors with a severely restricted range of grade levels. Data from this initiative shows that there is no meaningful correlation between course grades earned and the faculty ratings given by students at the end of a course.

Increasing Student Retention

Retention and graduation rates are long-term issues that are very dependent on procedures used to calculate the relevant data. NU, through the Office of Educational Effectiveness and Assessment, tracks student retention, persistence, and degree completion rates on an ongoing basis. It is important to note that 70% of the student body is composed of part-time students. As a result, time-to-degree completion for part-time students will necessarily be longer than for students who pursue their studies on a full-time basis.

Given the uniqueness of NU's academic structure and schedule, the university employs a format that approximates a traditional formula for computing retention and graduation rates. The traditional methodology, for example, determines that a regular load for undergraduate students is four courses per semester or quarter, and three courses per semester or quarter for graduate students. When this formula is applied to NU students, graduation rates over the past 10 years range from 65% to 75%.

In the fall of 2002, the Provost's Council and the Council of Chairs initiated a discussion on strategies intended to enhance the success of entering students. Strategies discussed included using a detailed analysis of retention and graduation rates by program and revisiting annual survey results to better understand why students leave the university. The focus was on whether students' decisions not to continue at NU are appropriate and desirable and on what the university can do to influence these decisions.

One strategy to improve retention was related to providing tutorials and support to assist students in achieving academic progress and success, particularly in such basic skills as writing. In 2000, the President's Commission on Writing developed and implemented several strategies to improve writing across the curriculum. Since then, faculty have adopted new program guidelines, and writing centers have been established at nearly all of the major academic centers around the state. In 2001, a director for the writing centers was appointed to connect with writing personnel and to coordinate the offering of faculty writing forums. Each year hundreds of faculty members attend these sessions, and the university also provides an online writing center.

Faculty and Staff

NU organizes and manages work and jobs according to its five major divisions, each of which is led by a provost or vice president. Consistent job descriptions and qualifications throughout the structure provide an equitable distribution of a qualified workforce. Currently, the university employs 216 faculty, 2,200 adjunct instructors, and 618 full- and part-time staff members. Statewide meetings ensure consistency and alignment in all aspects of regional operations. Employees at all operational levels meet annually to share information.

Faculty and Staff Performance Management Systems

NU has a performance-based compensation system for faculty and staff. There is no tenure system for faculty, and all senior level and staff administrators have annual contracts. Faculty and staff members are provided with multiple opportunities to participate in and contribute to the accomplishment of the university's strategic direction, as well as the chance to self-evaluate and recalibrate their levels of performance and contribution. The performance review cycle involves discussion of performance standards, suggests additional job and career-related learning objectives, and assesses expectations.

The faculty and staff performance management system supports high performance by ensuring that faculty and staff are hired with appropriate and verifiable credentials and experience; that they receive training/education to upgrade skills; that they establish and regularly review goals/objectives with their division, school, and/or department leaders as part of the annual performance appraisal and contract renewal process; and that they meet performance expectations. Individuals are rewarded for superior performance by promotion, merit pay, or other forms of recognition (see Figure 5.9).

Contract renewal and promotion are determined differently at NU than at most institutions of higher education. Many staff positions are designed as paid internal internships to ensure that students can apply learning in a business environment. Thus, the success of the educational programs is inversely related to retention rates of student staff members, who often move into the private sector when degree programs are completed. Nonstudent staff members are typically professionals who have had significant work experience.

Staff members develop annual goals and objectives and undergo a formal evaluation process with their supervisors. They are eligible for competitive annual merit increases based upon performance for individuals below the level of director or for the President's Player Award for superior performance. Recipients of this award receive an automatic 10% increase to their base salaries. Staff members who are not meeting performance expectations are subject to a progressive discipline policy, which may require that they receive additional training or mentoring. Employees who do not reach the level of "met expectations" in the performance

Figure 5.9

Means of Motivating Faculty and Staff at National University

Means	Internal Results or Processes
Increasing faculty and staff salaries	25% increase on average over past five years
Increasing faculty professional development stipend	50% increase in past five years
Midyear and end-of-year performance reviews	Ongoing encouragement and assistance
Lead faculty support/encouragement	Ongoing assistance in instructional-student matters
Participation on committees, commissions, and councils	Ongoing focus on issues that affect teaching and learning
Presidential awards	95% of applicants have received awards in the past 12 years
Employee Assistance Program	7% of employees used the program in 2002
Tuition Remission Program	An average of 135 employees used the program in 2002
Faculty promotion and merit system	Ensures that performance excellence is rewarded on a competitive basis
Director of sponsored research	Assists faculty in identifying grantors to fund research projects
Presidential Scholars Program (2001)	Release time for scholarly projects
President's Players Award (Est. 1999)	Awards staff for performance excellence

Means	Internal Results or Processes
Teacher of the Year Award (Est. 1992)	Ongoing recognition of teaching excellence
President's Bulldog Award (Est. 2002)	Ongoing recognition for employee tenacity
ARD Bridge Award	Recognition of faculty leadership

evaluation will receive a development plan created by their supervisor to enhance performance in the upcoming cycle.

The faculty performance evaluation system includes an annual review of dossiers that document individual performance for reappointment, promotion, and merit. Faculty merit ratings include a self-assessment rating that is linked to ratings by the department chair, the dean, the school personnel committee, the university personnel committee, the provost, and a final review by the president, ensuring that overall merit evaluations are reliable. Since no across-the-board or cost-of-living adjustments are provided, the merit system motivates faculty to achieve high performance ratings. The criteria for the faculty performance evaluation system also include student outcomes and student learning.

Faculty and Staff Learning and Motivation

The employee performance appraisal form requires supervisors to summarize activities such as special coaching, training, and special assignments that will be planned to develop each employee supervised and to help improve job performance during the next appraisal period. Overall, institutional education/training needs are identified at two levels: 1) school/department-level needs, linked to the goals and objectives of those units and the institution; and 2) individual-level needs, linked to licensure, certification, or professional disciplinary requirements.

Beginning at the organizational level, with the annual employee and student surveys and the assessment summit, departmental goals and individual action plans are created. For example, customer service was identified as an area for improvement in recent survey analysis. Human resources responded with workshops on service and dealing with difficult customers. Other relevant training has included new hire orientation, leadership, team building, progressive discipline, powerful presentations, coaching and communication, delivering quality customer service, dealing with difficult customers, time management, performance appraisals, and technology training on various software programs.

A biweekly orientation program was initiated for all benefits-eligible staff and faculty that includes mission, core values, policies and procedures, diversity, harassment prevention, technology systems, service fundamentals, and benefits. The orientation process also includes sessions for individual departments, such as the five-day development program "Advisor 101" for all new admissions advisors.

All new faculty members attend a faculty orientation designed to help new instructors with the demands of teaching within the institution's unique format. This orientation highlights university policies and procedures for writing learning outcomes, developing course outlines, identifying grading standards and systems, designing interactive strategies to engage students, teaching online courses, integrating technology into on-site course teaching, understanding adult learners, and achieving institutional goals and objectives.

Training is delivered in a number of formats to meet the needs of employees who are located throughout the state, including distance education (online or video conferencing) at on- and off-center workshops, and seminars and conferences facilitated by external trainers and consultants or by in-house faculty and staff. Additional university education or external professional training is supported by tuition reimbursement, on-the-job training, or traditional classroom instruction; online initiatives begin at the staff and faculty levels.

Application of appropriate levels of knowledge and skills is reinforced and, if necessary, remediated by supervisor observations and performance evaluations. At a minimum, formal performance assessments take place annually. Deans, chairs, and lead faculty observe and evaluate instructors for possible promotion and merit, as well as to suggest pedagogical and classroom management practices or the inclusion of additional or different content. Monthly student evaluations—reviewed carefully by deans and department chairs and used as part of the performance evaluation of faculty—also spotlight competencies and areas that need improvement. Staff knowledge and skills are demonstrated by carefully monitored job productivity, as assessed against key weekly and monthly division performance indicators and annually against results of the assessment summit.

Faculty and Staff Well-Being and Satisfaction

NU determined key factors that affect faculty and staff well-being, satisfaction, and motivation through benchmarking studies, tracking and categorizing grievances, and monitoring absenteeism rates and turnover. Examining participation in assemblies, on committees, and in governance processes revealed that contributions by faculty and staff on a yearly basis increased by 97% from 1997 to 2000. Other methods of measuring employee satisfaction include tracking the number of hours of special leave for community service.

Key factors have traditionally included the reward system—salary and benefits, evaluation procedures, collegial and job relations, participation or representation in governance, leadership, and the general work environment. Indicators that assess those and other factors are reviewed annually to ensure that departments can change or adjust them as appropriate. Data collected for the indicators are analyzed regularly, and analyses are presented to the university community at large and to individual departments at the assessment summit. These studies provide data segmented by gender, ethnicity, and job classification in order to assist human resources and other departments in understanding the needs of different groups of employees.

Faculty and staff well-being, satisfaction, and motivation are measured with both formal and informal evaluation methods. Formal measures include an annual quality of service survey of all employees, administrative reviews, peer reviews, self-assessments, and committee reports. More indirect measures are derived from grievances, turnover rates, absenteeism statistics, and informal discussions and communications. All of these indicators provide information that helps the institution assess immediate problems and anticipate future concerns. Many of the formal methods are tailored to the diverse workforce so that the information can be segmented into different categories and types.

Management of Academic and Support Processes

NU determines its learning-centered processes through an interplay of faculty and academic governance, administrative and staff input, and available and relevant internal and external data. Initiating or modifying a new program or process may begin at any point in the cycle. Multiple data sources are used to evaluate needs and expectations for new programs, including current and projected job market analysis, employer needs, student and alumni interests, and analysis of what the competition is doing. Based on this information, faculty, staff, students, alumni, and administrators propose new programs.

To initiate new degree programs, full-time faculty consult with part-time faculty and other stakeholders to develop curriculum and program rationale. For example, the Border Patrol participated in program development for criminal justice and forensic science, Sempra Energy provided advice for the business degree programs, Gateway Computers served as a partner for technology programs, and K–12 school districts provided site placement and evaluation data for education programs. In a recently strengthened procedure, key administrators provided input early in the process regarding the likely market viability of a proposed new program.

After review by school academic committees, the Undergraduate Council and Graduate Council review proposed degree programs. Alignment with university and school mission, employers' need for the program, the size of the potential student market, program objectives, expected learning outcomes, quality of the curriculum, impact on existing program offerings, and resource requirements are criteria utilized in the review process. The cycle time for program development is aligned with the university's core value of accelerated pace. In general, new programs are developed and implemented in approximately 12 months.

The curriculum development process ensures that all programs and offerings address student needs. Once a new degree program receives final approval, a lead faculty member is appointed and a group of appropriate external disciplinary advisors is selected. These advisors are contacted individually or as a group to provide external input on current discipline demands and support for the program; they might be corporate leaders in business or technology, superintendents of schools, or other individuals appropriate for the program. The lead faculty member guides the implementation, which involves distribution of program documentation on goals, objectives, and curriculum; faculty and staff development; and development of an assessment plan.

To ensure high standards in the implementation of the curriculum, NU has standardized course syllabi that outline prerequisites, performance objectives, and textbooks; recommended assignments, grading standards, and bibliographies; and recommended individual and group learning activities and evaluation criteria. The lead faculty member, the department chair, and the school dean determine the start date of the program at approved locations. Determination of appropriate locations for the programs is based on availability of faculty resources, student demand, and workforce needs in the area. In an environment that is so geographically dispersed, these processes provide standards and consistency to protect the integrity of the curriculum.

NU maintains a focus on active learning by including experiential learning activities that may involve group assignments, community involvement, qualitative research, synchronous and asynchronous online discussions, presentations, and the use of technology. All programs include a capstone course that requires students to actively integrate and apply the knowledge and skills gained in other courses, including student teaching and student portfolios.

Another key aspect of teaching and learning is online delivery of courses and programs. As of July 1, 2002, the National University System inaugurated a new component known as Spectrum Pacific Learning Company LLC. The primary responsibility of this entity is to provide consistent, high-quality implementation and delivery of course content authored and initiated by faculty members. Part of this new resource is a new determination to move as many courses and programs as possible to the online as well as on-site format, on the basis of constituent feedback regarding the need or desire for access to the online format.

Student Support Processes

Key support process requirements are determined by two primary methods: 1) needs assessment through the strategic planning and budget process, and 2) feedback from surveys and students and stakeholders (see Figure 5.10). Each year, administrators responsible for student service units identify needs and determine budget priorities in accordance with the strategic planning and budget development process. Results of student and staff surveys and assessment results have provided the impetus for budgeting additional resources in the areas of library access, technology laboratory access, and academic student support services. Essential support processes are determined by individual operating units. NU operates from the premise that individuals on the frontline are in the best position to determine vital support processes and the operational requirements needed to implement them. Daily operational processes are designed around overall targets and benchmarks. These targets and benchmarks naturally flow from the organizational performance review and the strategic planning and student survey processes.

Key performance measures/indicators used for the control and improvement of these processes include growth in enrollment, growth in the number of learning centers, growth in the number of full-time faculty, growth in the number of students using the writing center, increases in student satisfaction levels, increases in faculty and staff satisfaction levels, continued affordability of tuition, continuous improvement on a variety of external financial ratios and measures, continued growth in the endowment, improvements in the levels of sophistication and services provided by information technology teams, and continued enhancements to the library's electronic resources.

Improvement in student satisfaction rates is at the core of NU's mission and goes beyond monitoring transactions and reviewing survey data annually. The key performance indicators are measured for individual employees and for the unit as a whole in order to plan developmental opportunities and unit benchmarks for continuous quality improvement.

Figure 5.10

Support Service Process and Key Requirements at National University

Student Support Processes	Key Operational Requirements
Admissions	• New students contacted prior to start of first class • Appropriate scheduling • Accuracy of advising information • Prompt response to initial inquiries
Records and matriculation	• Timely and accurate assembly of records • Timely matriculation of students, especially those needing financial aid
Financial aid	• Complete and accurate financial aid advising • Timely financial aid processing
Credentials	• Accurate and appropriate advising processing and student teaching placements to meet state requirements
Assessment and academic assistance	• Placement of undergraduate students in writing and mathematics courses • Increased competencies in writing and math • Availability of writing center services
Online career advising	• Availability of career services
Library	• Access to information
Technology	• Access to technology resources

References

American Council on Education. (2002). *The American college president, 2002 edition*. Washington, DC: Author.

Lee, J. C. (1996). *National University: An environment of quality*. Presentation at the University Assembly, National University, La Jolla, CA.

Nichols, J. O. (1995). *Practitioner's handbook for institutional effectiveness and student outcomes assessment implementation*. New York, NY: Agathon Press.

Schwartz, D. (2002). *Student learning in accelerated college programs: A review of recent studies including CPA exam results*. La Jolla, CA: National University.

Serdyukov, P., Subbotin, I., & Serdyukova, N. (2002). *A one-subject, one-month model of intensive mathematics instruction and its implications on adult learners*. La Jolla, CA: National University.

Spitzer, T. M. (2000, Fall). Predictors of college success: A comparison of traditional and nontraditional age students. *NASPA Journal, 38*(1). Retrieved September 3, 2004, from http://publications.naspa.org/cgi/viewcontent.cgi?article=1130&context=naspajournal

Tatum, C., & Parker, J. (2002). *Concentrated versus extended learning: A comparison of two instructional formats*. La Jolla, CA: National University.

Zemke, R., & Zemke, S. (1984, March 9). 30 things we know for sure about adult learning. *Innovation Abstracts, 6*(8). Retrieved September 3, 2004, from http://honolulu.hawaii.edu/intranet/committees/FacDev Com/guidebk/teachtip/adults-3.htm

6

Northwest Missouri State University

Dean L. Hubbard, David C. Oehler

Founded in 1905 as a normal school to train teachers, Northwest Missouri State University has evolved into a comprehensive, state-assisted, regional university. Located in Maryville, the campus now offers 103 undergraduate degrees and 40 graduate degrees to its approximately 6,500 students. Northwest is a national leader in utilizing technology to deliver, improve, and accelerate learning, installing the nation's first comprehensive Electronic Campus in 1987. The institution's quality journey began in 1984, and the campus has participated in several Baldrige-based self-assessment programs at the state and national levels. Northwest received the Missouri Quality Award in 1997 and 2001. The following chapter describes the institution's quality improvement initiatives in the Baldrige categories.

Leadership Systems

Northwest Missouri State University embarked on its quality journey in 1984 when President Dean Hubbard presented a vision of an institution based on quality principles. A 25-member planning team formalized that vision into a 1987 document titled "The Culture of Quality," formalizing a commitment to continuous quality improvement that continues today.

The organizational structure that supports the institution's learning-centered focus consists of three leadership teams. The President's Cabinet, composed of the president, provost, five vice presidents, and two directors, is responsible for every facet of Northwest's operations. The Dean's Council, composed of the provost, six deans, three directors, and a department chair representative, is responsible for the development, delivery, and improvement of instruction and learning. The Strategic Planning Council, composed of the President's Cabinet, the Dean's Council, representatives from the Faculty Senate, the Support Staff Council, the Student Senate president, the student regent, and other campus leaders sets university directions, communicates high expectations for performance, and maintains a focus on learning.

Leadership Environment

Senior leaders are charged with the responsibility to create and maintain a climate that promotes empowerment, innovation, safety, equity, agility, learning, and legal and ethical behavior. Indeed, this charge is embedded in the institution's core values and vision statement. These expectations are implicit in each cabinet member's job responsibility and are part of the members' evaluations. Cabinet members are specifically trained to foster these attributes.

In the mid-1990s, the university president and a team of faculty leaders formally redesigned the governance process to encourage and facilitate agility and innovation for the teams. Job descriptions were written so that each leader's charge begins with providing support on the frontlines to encourage and sustain continuous improvement. As a result, the entire administrative structure was streamlined and realigned around continuous improvement and innovation.

As part of the streamlining process, budgetary control was decentralized to allow colleges and departments greater spending discretion. Faculty and staff were empowered to make changes to processes and procedures following a Seven-Step Planning Process (see Figure 6.1). Designed as a universal operational planning tool that is applied to university-level planning and to both academic and service units, the Seven-Step Planning

Process ensures that department and unit innovations are aligned with university key quality indicators (KQIs) and that a structured approach is followed for evaluation, progress tracking, identifying better practices, and setting performance goals. The Seven-Step Planning Process is fully deployed across campus, with every unit having completed at least three cycles. A manual and one-on-one support is provided to individuals or departments to assist in applying the process.

Figure 6.1

The Seven-Step Planning Process at Northwest Missouri State University

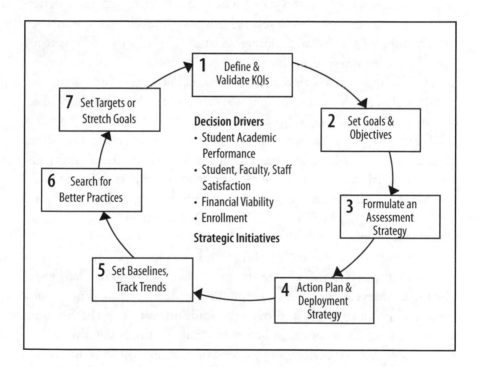

The entire process is built around organizational learning, with Steps 6 and 7 specifically focused on innovation. Innovations are funded through Culture of Quality grants and promote knowledge sharing through faculty showcases during board meetings and faculty assemblies. In order to stimulate ideas, teams of administrators and faculty regularly attend summer institutes sponsored by the Continuous Quality Improvement Network at companies like Saturn, Disney, Starbucks, Southwest Airlines, and 3M.

Organizational Performance Review

Northwest has developed a systematic structure for reviewing organizational performance. Senior leaders' reviews consist of a weekly President's Cabinet meeting, which includes a review of the president's dashboard measures (see Figure 6.2); a twice-monthly Dean's Council meeting, which includes a review of the provost's dashboard measures; and the bimonthly Strategic Planning Council meeting, which reviews progress to plan measures. The term "dashboard" refers to a data display of colored indicators that presents a real-time snapshot of the current status of key performance metrics relative to targets, including the aggregate performance and the highest and lowest performance in each group of metrics. Green and purple indicate performance at or above target. Yellow or red colors indicate when "drill-down" analysis is appropriate. Senior leaders share these indicators with their departments/units, who annually review the data along with specific student and stakeholder data that they collect as part of their own review processes.

Northwest's measurement system includes a set of critical measures that indicate overall organizational success across the decision drivers. Data gathered in support of the measurement system are analyzed, and the analysis includes comparisons to past performance, future goals, competitors, and other benchmarks, all of which are presented during the dashboard reviews.

Although the President's Cabinet and the Dean's Council initiates action to drive performance improvement when performance falls below the targeted levels, the primary forum for translating performance review results into priorities for improvement and innovation is the Strategic Planning Council meeting. When performance falls below the desired level, the leader responsible for that area or strategic initiative is required to identify alternatives to improve performance and present those alternatives at the Strategic Planning Council discussion.

Senior Leader Evaluation

The president is formally evaluated annually by the board, the cabinet, and the deans in areas of academic leadership and planning, budgetary and fiscal management, communication, decision-making and problem

Figure 6.2

President's Dashboard Measures and Review Findings at Northwest Missouri State University

Decision Driver	Dashboard Measure	Recent Review Findings
Enrollment	• Recruitment • Retention	• Green • Purple
Student success	• General education • Teacher education • Major field test • Freshman success • Graduation rate	• Green • Green • Purple • Green • Green
Satisfaction	• Student • Faculty • Staff	• Green • Green • Green
Financial performance	• Appropriations • Capital • Operations • Auxiliary • Fund balance • Endowment	• Purple • Purple • Purple • Purple • Yellow • Purple

solving, external relations, personnel, specific programs/initiatives, and interaction with the board. Faculty members also evaluate the president, provost, deans, and chairs annually. All members of the leadership team receive feedback for improvement through an annual goal-setting/performance review conference conducted by team leaders and supervisors. In turn, the leaders provide systematic, appropriate feedback to their departments/units to achieve continuous improvement. Further, faculty and staff satisfaction surveys and focus group results are analyzed to identify opportunities for leadership improvement.

As a group, senior leaders annually evaluate and improve the effectiveness of the leadership system during an annual cabinet planning retreat. Baldrige assessments and the Baldrige criteria have been used as a framework for reviewing performance and planning leadership improvements since 1993.

Support of Key Communities

In order to gauge the affect on the region, Northwest conducts studies on topics such as economic impact, the need for teacher in-service and graduate training opportunities, and satisfaction with Northwest graduates. The results of these studies are reviewed with the board and the Strategic Planning Council. Where appropriate, committees with regional representation assist in planning and policy reviews. Community leaders are integrated into planning activities such as the Strategic Planning Council's annual process for updating the Environmental Scan.

Northwest identifies key communities and determines areas for involvement during the annual planning retreat. Programs and services that will further the institution's emphasis on agriculture, business, and education are targeted. Northwest is a member of several organizations formed to strengthen the local community and the region. Campus leaders meet regularly with community leaders and serve in leadership roles in a range of community/region improvement activities. Examples include a regional healthy communities project, regional airport development, downtown renewal, and alternative crops development.

To better serve lifelong learners, Northwest operates the McKemy Center for Lifelong Learning, which houses programs serving professional groups in the community, region, and state in a state-of-the-art facility. Consulting services for small businesses are provided through the Small Business Development Center. Northwest is a member of three national consortia to share/collaborate on improving the overall quality of higher education. In addition, the campus has taken a leadership role in promoting continuous quality improvement in academia through hosting visitors, making national presentations, and contributing to numerous publications.

Strategic Planning

The Northwest Quality Systems Model (NQSM), shown in Figure 6.3, guides Northwest's strategy and action plan development process. The Strategic Planning Council is responsible for implementing the NQSM. Participants include representatives of the entire university community, plus key partners and other stakeholders. The NQSM produces the following strategic components: 1) decision drivers that provide long-term focus for the entire university, 2) strategic KQIs that establish long-term requirements in each of the decision driver areas, 3) strategic initiatives that specify focus areas and actions within the strategic KQIs, 4) tactical KQIs that specify requirements needed to achieve the strategic initiatives within each university department, and 5) action plans within each department to achieve the requirements of the tactical KQIs.

The decision drivers and strategic KQIs reach out to four years and beyond, the strategic initiatives and tactical KQIs are typically two to four years in duration, and the action plans are normally one-year activities. This methodology promotes alignment among the university departments by linking the short-term annual action plans with the long-term university objectives. The NQSM itself has been honed through improvement cycles.

Phase 1: Strategic Context

Strategic planning teams are formed to gather and analyze data in specific areas of importance. Northwest's mission, vision, and cultural core values are included as part of the communications sent to the strategic planning teams to emphasize the need to be student centered, to focus on a culture of quality that supports continuous improvement, and to take advantage of technological advances. These teams are responsible for providing information that forms the foundation needed to make important strategic decisions.

The first data source is the Environmental Scan, which focuses outwardly on external trends, data, and educational issues to ensure that Northwest understands its position in state, national, and global contexts. Currently, the Environmental Scan is conducted each year and reviews the following six areas: demographic, economic, technological, political/legal, social, and competitive. This process is conducted by teams of

Figure 6.3
The Quality Systems Model at Northwest Missouri State University

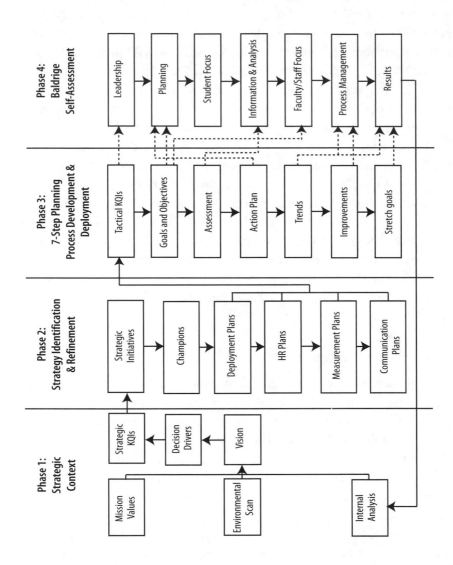

experts in each of these areas who compile trends and facts about each area and summarize them in broader, more encompassing statements called "megatrends." The megatrends are used by the "Voices to Access" at the Strategic Planning Council retreat to shape the planning and prioritizing process.

The second data source is an Internal Analysis, primarily based on Baldrige feedback, which not only details the university's strengths and weaknesses, but also includes feedback from the Missouri Department of Higher Education, accrediting agencies, stakeholders, and satisfaction and performance data. This information is used to define the position of Northwest relative to its foundational principles and external competition. Student achievement and student and stakeholder satisfaction are major areas of focus.

These data sources form the basis of the Strategic Context. Each of the megatrends, when combined with the Internal Analysis feedback and the wide range of representation during the Strategic Planning Council retreat, produces the necessary external and internal analyses needed to make sound planning decisions. All of this information is reviewed and discussed by the Strategic Planning Council and retreat participants when working through the NQSM model and selecting strategic initiatives.

Northwest develops strategic KQIs for each of the four decision drivers. The current strategic plan includes strategic educational KQIs, strategic service KQIs, strategic enrollment KQIs, and strategic financial KQIs.

Phase 2: Strategy Identification and Refinement

The strategic key quality indicators are reviewed by the Strategic Planning Council during Phase 2 of the NQSM. The council creates a possible list of strategic initiatives from the Environmental Scan megatrends and the Internal Analysis, and filters them through the decision drivers. The proposed strategic initiatives are reviewed and validated during subsequent retreats. The current seven strategic initiatives and their corresponding goals, actions, and measures are shown in Figure 6.4.

A "champion" is responsible for the implementation of each strategic initiative and oversees the development of four interlocking plans: 1) a Deployment Plan, 2) a Human Resources Plan, 3) a Measurement Plan, and 4) a Communications Plan. The Deployment Plan details the specific

Figure 6.4

The Strategic Plan at Northwest Missouri State University

Decision Drivers/KQIs	Strategic Initiatives	Goals (Actions)	Measures
Enrollment • Enrollment KQIs	Enrollment management	• Expand catchment area with KC focus • ID and recruit gifted high school students for academy • Attract underrepresented groups • Serve place-bound learners • Develop graduate programs in niche markets	# of Kansas City students # of FTE students % of freshmen meeting standards # of new markets
	Diversity	• Improve marketing and recruitment of underrepresented groups • Increase intercultural experiences for students • Align diversity plan • Establish partnerships in urban schools • Refine support structure to meet minority/international student needs • Foster an environment of inclusion • Provide high-quality academic and cultural study-abroad programs	% of minority and international students Undergraduate recruitment # Graduate recruitment #

Decision Drivers/KQIs	Strategic Initiatives	Goals (Actions)	Measures
Student success • Educational KQIs	Integrating technology	• Provide electronic portfolio for students • Increase faculty participation in development of active, accelerated, modularized, and anytime/anywhere learning • Develop online student services • Collaborate with other Missouri institutions in developing online courses • Develop sufficient software/server capacity • Develop adult learner's advisement program	Percentage of students above 50th percentile—general education (target: 60%) Freshman success rate Six-year graduation rate (CBHE target: 55%) Teacher education composite score (target: 60%) Percentage of students above 50th percentile—major field exams (target: 60%)
	Teacher education	• Reframe teacher preparation program • Become key provider of teachers and staff for urban schools • Develop innovations for addressing teacher shortages, retention in first three years, and continuing education • Provide student experiences in urban schools	

continued on page158

Decision Drivers/KQIs	Strategic Initiatives	Goals (Actions)	Measures
Satisfaction • Educational KQIs • Service KQIs	Human Resources	• Use market data for setting salary trends • Pilot competency-based work/job design • Pilot the Kirkpatrick evaluation model • Adopt the two-year cycle for market-based internal adjustments	Student satisfaction Faculty satisfaction Staff satisfaction
	Communication (centennial celebration)	• Develop systems to facilitate two-way communications • Increase publicity about Northwest in trend markets • Create media resources • Involve employees in community activities • Plan celebration for 2005–2006	Online student satisfaction
Financial • Financial KQIs	Financial flexibility	• Increase indebtedness fund balance • Increase participation of alumni and friends in activities • Increase alumni and corporate giving • Integrate SSPP with Q/ABC	Appropriations Capital Auxiliary Fund balance Endowment Foundation fund

goals and activities that will be used to achieve the strategic initiative. The Human Resources Plan details the personnel requirements that will be needed. The Measurement Plan establishes a baseline, a two-year projection, and a five-year projection. The Communications Plan describes who (both externally and internally) will be informed about the strategic initiative and how this information will be communicated.

Phase 3: Seven-Step Planning Process Development and Deployment

Once strategic initiatives have been established, they are implemented and sustained at the department, unit, and individual levels through the Seven-Step Planning Process. Tactical KQIs are derived from the Deployment, Human Resources, Measurement, and Communications Plans of the strategic initiative and reflect the goals that each department/unit must achieve to successfully implement the action plans. The Seven-Step Planning Process requires that each level of the organization establish objectives, assess performance, identify action plans, track performance, identify improvement priorities, and set performance goals.

Financial resources are allocated to strategic initiatives at both the university and department levels. The process begins with the cabinet, where funds are allocated during a series of budget-focused meetings held after the annual Strategic Planning Council retreat. Since the academic budget is decentralized, the academic deans are empowered to add funds at the department level to ensure that necessary resources are available to support the tactical KQI requirements identified within each department.

Phase 4: Baldrige Self-Assessment

Northwest has conducted self-assessments using the Baldrige criteria seven times between 1994 and 2003. The feedback that results from this process is utilized extensively in Phase 1 of the strategic planning process. The combination of feedback from the formal Baldrige assessment process, third-party scoring, and internal analysis results in a wealth of potential improvement information, which feeds back into Phase 1 and drives numerous initiatives and improvement action plans.

Market, Student, and Stakeholder Focus

The strategic planning process includes an environmental scan that identifies trends that affect the campus and its market position. To identify appropriate markets, data gathered from census reports, ACT and College Board-supplied market analyses, focus groups, and national surveys of prospective college students are reviewed. From these data, market segments are identified, including potential segments. Segments (see Figure 6.5) are defined as groups that require special accommodation at some point during their interaction with Northwest. The individual colleges also segment students according to class standing and major field of study.

The ACT Enrollment Information Service and the College Board Survey identify feeder schools, compute yield rates, and calculate the market potential of students who meet admission standards. These data are synthesized and converted into marketing and financial aid strategies to attract students who might go elsewhere. The dean of enrollment management generates weekly reports that compare recruiting results for each segment with previous years' results. This information is shared with the President's Cabinet, the Dean's Council, and the Strategic Planning Council and leads to mid-course corrections or new initiatives for targeting specific student segments.

Understanding Student Needs

In order to understand the key requirements and expectations of prospective students, the campus gathers and analyzes data from prospective students through the ACT Information Manager, College Board surveys, new student surveys, and parent surveys. Students who apply and are admitted but fail to matriculate are contacted. Additionally, admissions representatives regularly visit feeder high schools, participate in college fairs, and communicate with feeder school guidance counselors. Through these ongoing interactions, feedback is received and integrated into the segment-specific recruiting plan.

The listening and learning system is comprehensive, multifaceted, and longitudinal. In addition to feedback gained through national surveys and databases, a variety of locally developed listening posts provide information regarding student requirements and expectations. Individual departments, such as the Counseling Center, send surveys to their clients. Short

Figure 6.5

Sample Student Segments and Key Requirements Used by Northwest Missouri State University

Students	Key Requirements
Transfer	• Focused orientation • Course articulation
Minority	• Respect for diversity • Opportunities to express identity
Resident	• Work opportunities • Social interaction and engagement
Off-campus	• Access to technology • Space for social interaction • Parking
International	• Visa processing • Focused orientation • Opportunities to express identity
At-risk	• Academic support • Advising
Online	• Technical support

surveys are posted regularly on the Electronic Campus to quickly measure student preferences regarding a wide range of topics. (The Electronic Campus consists of a system of networked computers in residence hall rooms and offices on campus, as well as several special use labs.)

The needs of nontraditional students are assessed through a special section of Freshman Seminar, as well as through frequent interaction with the Association of Nontraditional Students. Student affairs administrators serve as advisors to the Student Senate, attend weekly senate meetings, and follow up on concerns. Student media also provide additional forums for students to communicate about the quality of services provided and initiatives being considered, and the student regent maintains a web site where students may raise issues and post questions.

Through new student orientation and a required Freshman Seminar, students become active participants in their educational experience and take responsibility for planning their futures. Through the Covenant for Learning (a pact between students and Northwest), the students' and the university's responsibilities are articulated, and each "pledges" to do what is necessary to ensure student success. Freshmen are expected to develop individualized first-year success plans, and student programming in the freshman residence halls and Freshman Seminar coursework are fully integrated. As students progress through their programs, they interact with their advisors and are involved in student organizations and campus-life experiences.

Understanding Stakeholder Needs

Northwest's primary stakeholders include employers, graduate schools, alumni, the state Coordinating Board for Higher Education (CBHE), and the local community and region (see Figure 6.6). The KQI identification and validation step of the Seven-Step Planning Process is the principal method used to understand and monitor stakeholder requirements. This step involves receiving input from advisory groups, and through surveys, focus groups, and other stakeholder interactions in order to ensure KQIs are appropriate. The listening posts for monitoring stakeholder requirements are similar to those for students.

Academic departments have advisory boards/councils that provide valuable insight about changes in their respective career categories. Departments monitor their graduates' acceptance rate into and subsequent success in graduate schools, and utilize membership in professional organizations to address changes in academic preparation necessary for graduate education and/or employment. Alumni requirements are solicited through the ACT Alumni Outcomes Survey, the Northwest Foundation Board, during alumni chapter meetings, and through the alumni

Figure 6.6

Stakeholder Groups and Key Requirements at Northwest Missouri State University

Key Stakeholder	Key Requirements
Employers	• Qualified internship/job candidates
Graduate schools	• Qualified candidates
Alumni	• Information about Northwest • Networking opportunities • Opportunities for involvement • Objects of pride (sports, etc.)
CBHE	• Alignment with state plans/initiatives • Positive trends on CBHE measures
Community/region	• Economic development • Learning opportunities • Community development

magazine. The Small Business Development Center surveys businesses and industries to identify regional education needs. Faculty members also conduct economic impact studies and monitor national trends and feed this information into the planning process. The director of assessment, information, and analysis works with campus leaders to systematically review all instruments and surveys. The campus watches the marketplace and changes or upgrades national surveys when improvements are made.

Complaint Management

Employees at Northwest are acculturated to elicit feedback from students and stakeholders and to respond, as appropriate, to complaints. When possible, an employee is expected to resolve a complaint; when it is beyond his or her capacity to do so, an employee reports the problem to the appropriate unit leader to address. The comment card system is the primary complaint management mechanism. Students are encouraged by faculty and staff to use comment cards to share ideas or to register complaints. The majority of student complaints, approximately 25 per week, are received through comment cards. The cards are sent to the president's office where they are recorded, acknowledged within 48 hours, and then forwarded to the appropriate unit. The complaint is then investigated and a response is formulated. After a complaint has been addressed at the cabinet or department/unit level, a cabinet member reports back to the president's office about the method of response and actions taken.

Determining Student and Stakeholder Satisfaction

Student satisfaction is determined by use of the Noel-Levitz Student Satisfaction Inventory at the freshmen and junior levels, transfer orientation survey, transfer first-year experience evaluation, Junior Class Survey, Student Opinionnaires of Teaching, Resident Satisfaction Survey, and other measures. The campus also regularly conducts focus groups to obtain more descriptive information about student and stakeholder satisfaction.

Satisfaction of employers and graduate schools is measured and tracked through the use of surveys, focus groups, graduate school admissions, and advisory groups. The board of regents and CBHE maintain formal communication channels through regular meetings with the president and the cabinet. In addition to feedback received from the ACT Alumni Outcomes Survey, feedback from alumni is obtained from the Northwest Foundation and Alumni Association boards.

Student and stakeholder satisfaction data are systematically analyzed and displayed on cabinet members' dashboards. Cabinet members share these indicators with their units, which annually review the data along with specific student and stakeholder data that are collected as part of the plan. Satisfaction results from cabinet member dashboards are also reviewed during Strategic Planning Council meetings.

Measurement, Analysis, and Knowledge Management

The Seven-Step Planning Process drives the measurement system requirements. It serves as a conceptual framework and template for determining requirements, selecting performance measures, identifying best practices, and setting performance goals. Step 3 of the process calls for the formulation of an assessment strategy to monitor formative and summative measures and indicators. In this step, the unit selects appropriate data for each of the KQIs identified in Steps 1 and 2 of the Seven-Step Planning Process, and specifies when and how the data are to be collected and analyzed for support of decision-making.

A further description of the integration of information and processes to the larger educational system is addressed in the annual report process, which is strongly aligned with the Seven-Step Planning Process. For each KQI, consideration is given to the point in the process where assessment is done, to the need for repeating assessments on an appropriate cycle, to ensuring that assessment results are forwarded to someone with assigned responsibility, and to specifying appropriate and inappropriate uses of the data. Information related to daily operations is tracked at the departmental level, whereas overall institutional performance information is tracked through the dashboard system. A mix of data types for KQIs is used, including performance measures, satisfaction measures, and cost measures.

The balanced scorecard approach is used as a tracking tool; a dashboard model has been developed for summarizing balanced scorecard information. This system is used at the department level up through the institutional level to monitor organizational performance and support decision-making. Dashboards are aligned with key processes and reviewed on a regular basis by various decision-making groups and as part of the formal annual report process.

In addition to dashboard data, units develop formative measures to provide a more detailed short-cycle picture of the processes being assessed. Formative measures are used in the analysis of daily operations and to modify work in progress. Formative data are used by individual faculty members, program coordinators, and curriculum teams within a department and are not reported in the dashboard system. However, these data might play a significant role in a drill-down of less than satisfactory results indicated at the summative level.

Actual performance data are entered into the dashboard system by the heads of reporting units, and aggregated results are generated throughout the system through the use of linked spreadsheets and databases, allowing for real-time data availability. The Office of Assessment, Information, and Analysis manages the structure for dashboard data. The main types of information and data used to drive and track educational progress are outcomes and performance data, satisfaction ratings, and operational effectiveness data.

Use of Comparative Data

The Seven-Step Planning Process is also used to identify comparative data requirements and sources of comparative data. External comparative data are used wherever relevant data are available. When external comparisons are not possible, methods such as trend analysis and internal comparisons are employed. Criteria for the selection of targets for comparative data include three sources: 1) the source is a member of a comparative group, 2) the source is best in class, and/or 3) the source has comparable measures/indicators. Nationally normed instruments are used for comparative data whenever appropriate. In many cases, industry standard comparative data are used. In other cases, consortia for data exchange are used.

Based on feedback obtained through the Baldrige assessment process, Northwest engaged an independent, third-party consultant to select a set of peer institutions for comparative purposes. This method identified 41 peer institutions. Since many of these institutions do not use the same tests, comparative data on student performance come from Missouri competitors.

At the dashboard level, relevant comparative data are displayed with the most recent Northwest data. For student performance data, comparisons are made with direct competitors, while student satisfaction results are compared to the 41 peer institutions. The cabinet members evaluate the information and determine appropriate performance targets. Regardless of the method used, a mathematical analysis comparing actual performance to target performance is conducted, and a numeric indicator is generated. Where multiple indicators are aggregated into a single overall metric, each contributing metric is assigned a weighting. The overall weighted metric is then used to create the dashboard display. Contributing metrics are also analyzed in order to create an indicator showing when drill-down analysis is needed.

Performance Analysis

Depending on the source of data, various types of analyses are performed to support senior leaders' review of organizational performance. School performance and capabilities are reviewed to assess progress through the use of trend charts (academic performance and satisfaction), Pareto analysis (comment cards), Gantt charts (key events), histograms (service performance), affinity diagrams (environmental scanning), and modified control charts (budget monitoring). Predictive relationships are used in financial planning. For example, enrollment history and projections are used to calculate appropriate tuition and fee rates. Cause and effect relationships are explored through the annual report process as department/unit leaders interpret results and discuss these conclusions with senior leaders.

Overall performance is summarized in the president's dashboard (shown earlier in Figure 6.2). In some cases, data are disaggregated before analysis (student performance segmented by major), while in other cases data are aggregated for analysis (overall student performance). Overall group data are reported as summative information on dashboards, and individual student performance data are reported as formative/operational information to faculty and students. Financial data are analyzed monthly. Minter ratios are used for comparative analysis of expenditure patterns, looking at national and peer group norms. Institutions that appear to be performing better than Northwest are identified and may be used as benchmarks.

Appropriation funding is compared to other Missouri public, four-year regional institutions. Faculty salaries are compared to those of other Masters I institutions participating in the College and University Personnel Association (CUPA) salary study as well as to similar state institutions. Staff and administrative salaries are compared to appropriate survey comparison groups such as the national Watson Wyatt or CUPA surveys. These data are reviewed on a regular cycle in Strategic Planning Council meetings. Organization-level analysis related to strategic planning is distributed to participants as part of the planning process. Organizational-level analysis is also tied back to units through the annual report process. Cabinet members provide feedback on support units in the annual reports. In academic departments, annual report follow-up visits include identification and discussion of institution-wide and department-specific successes and concerns.

Information and Knowledge Management

Appropriate data and information, including dashboards, are available to faculty, staff, and administrators through the Electronic Campus. Protection levels are set to regulate improper or accidental updates to the data and to control access from the individual level through total campus access. Dashboards are user friendly in a Microsoft Excel spreadsheet; faculty and staff only need to select the dashboard storage system and follow hyperlinks to their dashboard to quickly see their data in easy-to-read graphical form. Information for other populations is distributed through various standard reports, newsletters, local newspaper articles, reports, and publications. Almost any data can be retrieved, compared, and analyzed from the extensive student, employee, and financial record systems by the data processing department.

The Computer Users Group meets regularly to provide input for acquiring, prioritizing, and aligning data and information mechanisms. This group, composed of professional and administrative staff from offices that rely heavily on the computing system for daily operations, reviews data and information availability in terms of service needs and directions. The group reviews emerging needs with staff, prioritizes improvement proposals, explores whether new software should be purchased, and suggests improvements to data systems.

This group also does long-range planning for data architecture needs and identifies the changing data needs of faculty, students, and other stakeholders. The client/server department monitors new software releases and patches, which support more reliable and secure information systems. Students and faculty are regularly surveyed to track their changing needs for computing resources and vote their approval of new systems. Faculty notebook computers are refreshed every three years and student systems every four years. The original Electronic Campus (1987) has evolved from a terminal system to a PC system to a notebook computer system.

Best practices and improvements are identified and shared in several ways. The continuous improvement culture encourages everyone to look for improvement opportunities. Continuous improvement is reinforced by the monitoring of results in the dashboard system, by discussion of trends and activities in annual reports, by feature articles in "Northwest

This Week," and by other recognition activities. In addition, Northwest conducts a day-long Celebration of Quality to reinforce the sharing of new knowledge and best practices. Further performance improvements are acknowledged in formal review processes.

Faculty and Staff Focus

Northwest is organized around discipline-based academic departments, administrative and academic support functions, student affairs, information technology, communications and marketing, and institutional advancement. Cabinet members lead these areas and are charged with ensuring that the university's culture and core values are brought to life in their units. Each work unit has a mission, goals, and objectives that are aligned with the university's strategic plan and refined following the Seven-Step Planning Process. Plans are updated and performance is reviewed annually. The decentralized decision-making structure and focus on shared governance promotes empowerment and fosters agility and innovation.

Although organized by function, Northwest has a strong team-based culture built around cooperation and collaboration. Work is typically performed in one of the following team environments:

- **Work-center teams,** which are generally self-directed and empowered to share responsibilities, initiate cross-training, improve processes, make decisions, and recruit other individuals and teams who might contribute to the success of their work

- **Cross-functional teams,** which bring different areas together to communicate across department lines and solve problems, plan events, improve processes, and provide feedback

- **Ad hoc teams,** which are formed as needed to collaborate in goal-setting and problem-solving activities.

Performance Management System

Northwest uses two methods to manage performance: Career Pathing and the Seven-Step Planning Process. Career Pathing emphasizes development, feedback, and cooperative goal setting, using coaching and mentoring by faculty and staff leaders to focus on high performance and achievement of personal and organizational goals. The Seven-Step Planning Process begins with a focus on student and stakeholder needs and integrates quality concepts into all processes. Both methods are decentralized to the department/unit level.

Currently, Career Pathing is fully deployed among the faculty and partially deployed to the staff. The faculty program includes guidelines and procedures for rank and promotion, a mentoring guidebook, and provisions for constructive feedback. All faculty members are evaluated every trimester by their students and annually by their chair, with the exception of tenured full professors who are evaluated on a three-year cycle. Tenure-track faculty members are mentored for seven years and receive special reviews after their third and fifth years.

Team performance against KQIs is assessed annually. Faculty, administrative, and professional leaders are given feedback based on their contributions to the overall goals of the university and achievement of their departmental KQIs. Support staff members are provided feedback based on evaluations of their performance pertaining to their specific duties and responsibilities and their individual and team-related contributions to department goals. Since the KQIs are focused on high performance and student and stakeholder needs and feedback is directly tied to how well faculty and staff meet their KQIs, this method of managing performance supports high organizational performance and achievement of short- and long-term organizational goals.

Northwest uses a market-based compensation system that attracts and retains top-quality faculty and staff, using national salary data for all work groups, targeting 90% to 110% of appropriate market medians. The recognition program emphasizes high-performance work and student and stakeholder focus through a variety of awards, recognition events, and publications. Individual and team presentations and/or research are recognized on web sites that are accessible to the campus and the community.

Hiring and Career Progression

Professionals in each department determine the characteristics and skills needed by potential faculty. Key performance requirements are written into job postings and used for applicant screening for faculty and staff positions. The interviewing process focuses specifically on service interests and capabilities, cultural core values, willingness to use technology, and on department/unit KQIs.

In the summer of 2000, senior leaders benchmarked the "Disney way" of integrating new employees into and reinforcing an organization's culture. Based on that experience, the campus implemented improvements in recruitment and selection, employee orientation, communication methods, recognition programs, and events that support the desired culture. Orientation starts with an overview of the core values and includes an introduction to the NQSM and Seven-Step Planning Process.

Northwest has a systematic succession plan (Leadership Development Plan) that was formally adopted by the board of regents. The plan involves selecting a small pool of candidates from the faculty and staff who participate in training, shadowing, and mentoring for one year. The objective is to create a pool of qualified candidates for a wide range of positions when they become open. On an annual basis the board reviews performance to ensure that the campus is ready to fill senior positions when they occur, either through retirement or resignation. Half of the current senior leaders were promoted from within. In order to encourage employee development, Northwest provides release time and 100% tuition reimbursement for all employees.

Training, Education, and Development

Phase 2 of the NQSM, Strategy Identification and Refinement, requires strategic initiative champions to develop human resource plans along with deployment plans, measurement plans, and communication plans. This step directly links education and training to the key needs arising from action plans. Learning requirements identified through this process are integrated into an annual in-service training plan built around four sequential questions,

- What outcomes do we want to achieve?

- What learning activities do we have to facilitate to produce those outcomes?

- What is the most efficient way to organize to deliver the training?

- How will we evaluate the effectiveness of the whole process?

Training that targets large segments of the faculty and/or staff always focuses on some aspect of the Culture of Quality. Desired outcomes can usually be grouped under four headings: 1) implementing or pilot testing a new tool, technique, or program, 2) improving current performance (writing across the curriculum, improving customer service delivery), 3) better understanding of existing or new processes (measuring student engagement, budget development and control), and 4) information sharing.

The third step in the process—organization—is addressed after the necessary activities have been identified. If the learning involves curricular issues, the provost is responsible for organizing and evaluating the actual delivery of instruction. Similarly, if the activity involves student services, the vice president for student affairs is in charge. The human resources office coordinates new employee orientation, all Strategic Planning Council training, student worker training, and general quality training. The Center for Information Technology in Education delivers training for the application of technology to educational processes. Computing Services coordinates training relating to hardware and software applications.

Success in achieving its quality goals is the benchmark against which Northwest measures the effectiveness of training. The dashboard provides the metrics. Additionally, at the end of every training activity, participants are surveyed to determine the appropriateness and effectiveness of the training. Depending on the nature of the training, overall effectiveness is measured by participation rates, participant satisfaction, learning, application to the work environment, and impact on overall quality.

Faculty and Staff Well-Being and Satisfaction

Two approaches are used for determining key factors that affect well-being, satisfaction, and motivation. One addresses the faculty; the other addresses the staff. The faculty used a collaborative process to identify their most important satisfiers so that their annual satisfaction survey could be constructed to focus on those issues. Each year after the survey has been completed, the leadership of the Faculty Senate, in consultation with the provost, evaluates the results, refines the list of key factors as appropriate, and publishes a "State of the Faculty" overview of the survey results, which identifies issues that will be jointly addressed.

To survey support staff, professional staff, and administrators, the Human Resources Advisory Council selected a Noel-Levitz Campus Quality Survey as the method to determine key satisfiers because the results could be segmented and the survey aligned with the Noel-Levitz Student Satisfaction Inventory. The key factors and priorities for staff well-being, motivation, and satisfaction are derived through gap analysis using this survey tool.

Satisfaction results are rolled up and analyzed by the provost, the vice president for finance, and the human resources director in order to identify opportunities for improving faculty satisfaction and morale. Results are reviewed by the cabinet and presented to the Strategic Planning Council. When appropriate, strategic initiatives are developed to ensure that improvements are made. Recent examples of changes driven by survey results include enhanced technology support, a change in health insurance, and workshops on student advising.

Process Management

Northwest's learning-centered processes are an outgrowth of the university's mission and include instruction and student services. Northwest uses its Seven-Step Planning Process to determine, design, and deliver educational processes and to improve existing processes. Every process has a matrix that includes the following (also shown in Figure 6.1):

- Defines and validates KQIs

- Sets goals and objectives

- Formulates an assessment strategy

- Defines action plans and a deployment strategy

- Sets baselines and tracks trends and comparisons

- Searches for better practices

- Sets targets and stretch goals

In addition, cost analysis activities, such as determining the unit cost of resources and calculating the cost of assessment, are also defined.

The design and delivery of new educational programs and offerings, along with the evaluation and improvement of existing programs, demonstrates how the Seven-Step Planning Process is such an integral part of Northwest's learning-centered processes. During Phase 1 of the NQSM, the campus identifies opportunities for developing new programs and/or the need to modify current offerings. Typically, a faculty team is formed to develop a proposal that includes student and market demand, societal need, program structure, assessment and delivery methods, financial projections, and accreditation requirements. As the team proceeds with Steps 1 through 4 of the Seven-Step Planning Process, team members seek input from stakeholders and proceed through the formal program approval channels.

Determining Key Learning-Centered Process Requirements

The strategic educational KQIs reflect the requirements of the instructional learning-centered processes (see Figure 6.7). Northwest ensures that these requirements are met by applying the Seven-Step Planning Process to every program offering. The process is used by all academic departments and ensures a tight linkage among KQIs, course design, achievement measurement, and improvement cycles.

Primary student service providers include enrollment services, the library, student affairs, information management (computing), academic assistance, and the Center for Information Technology in Education. Key requirements for these services are determined using the Seven-Step Planning Process in the same manner that educational program requirements are determined (see Figure 6.8). The process ensures that student/stakeholder input is obtained in the development of KQIs and then validated with users.

Assessment and Improvement of Instruction and Student Service Processes

To evaluate general education and major program knowledge, summative student achievement measures are used, including the Academic Profile, Major Field Tests, senior performances, portfolios, and locally developed assessments. Most courses include quizzes, tests, written papers, presen-

Figure 6.7

Key Instruction Processes, Requirements, and Measures at Northwest Missouri State University

Learning-Centered Processes	Requirements (KQIs)	Measures
Instruction	*Educational KQIs*	*Student Achievement Measures*
Curriculum	Computer competencies	• Using computer indicators • Alumni Outcomes Survey • Computer Competencies Survey
	Competence in a discipline	• Major field tests • Local major field indicators • Employer ratings • Junior Class Survey • Alumni Outcomes Survey
Teaching/advising	Communications competencies	• English composition assessment • Academic profile sub-score • Alumni Outcomes Survey
	Critical/creative thinking and problem-solving competencies	• Academic profile sub-score • Alumni Outcomes Survey
	Self-directed learning competencies	• NSSE • Junior Class Survey • Alumni Outcomes Survey

continued on page 176

Learning-Centered Processes	Requirements (KQIs)	Measures
Learning environment	Personal/social development	• NSSE • Junior Class Survey • Alumni Outcomes Survey
	Teamwork/team leading competencies	• NSSE • Alumni Outcomes Survey
	Multicultural competencies	• NSSE • Alumni Outcomes Survey
	Cultural enrichment	• NSSE • Alumni Outcomes Survey

tations, group projects, case study analyses, and other assignments that provide more timely, formative assessments. Courses are evaluated at their conclusion and in many instances at the mid-point by students. This process occurs once a trimester in each course taught by untenured faculty and annually in each course taught by tenured professors.

In the spring of 2004, a task force was created to examine student success in teacher preparation programs. The goal was to determine the characteristics of students who were successful in meeting the state certification requirements and the characteristics of students who achieved a high score on the relevant teacher certification content exam. A cross-functional team examined student demographic and academic achievement data and developed a predictive model for student success on these two outcomes.

Experience indicated that many students who want to be teachers do not meet the threshold levels for some of the predictive variables, so an array of intrusive student support programs was designed to customize help for each student. For example, students with low reading scores are channeled into college reading courses and test-taking workshops to develop a skill set that will help them when taking the required standardized tests and improve their knowledge retention from course reading

Figure 6.8
Student Services, Service Key Quality Indicators, and Performance Measures at
Northwest Missouri State University

Student Services	Requirements (KQIs)	Measures
*Enrollment** Recruitment, admissions, registration, financial assistance, career services, SOAR	• Treating you with respect, fairness, and honesty • Performing tasks with competence and skill	• Student satisfaction • Sub-process-specific measures
Library Collections/resources, instruction, instructional support	• Communicating clearly and courteously the services provided	• Student satisfaction • Sub-process-specific measures
Student Affairs Residential life, campus activities, health center, counseling center	• Listening actively to requests, comments, and concerns	• Student satisfaction • Sub-process-specific measures
Information Management (Computing) Help desk, computer labs, residence halls, instructors, classrooms, remote facilities	• Being flexible and open to new ideas • Providing what we agree to deliver in a timely manner	• Student satisfaction • Faculty and staff satisfaction • Sub-process-specific measures
Academic Assistance Supplemental instruction, student athlete success, talent development center, student support services, upward bound, writing center	• Maintaining a safe, orderly, healthy, well-functioning, and attractive campus	• Student satisfaction • Sub-process-specific measures
CITE Faculty notebooks, modular learning, web-based courses		• Student satisfaction • Faculty and staff satisfaction • Process-specific measures

*The enrollment KQIs apply to this process.

assignments. Where students with at-risk entrance scores have little prior experience in specific required content areas, coursework is directed to fill knowledge gaps so that students have the appropriate background to succeed on standardized tests. The current process identifies students who are at-risk and provides individualized assistance to help prevent failure and ensure success.

Over time, the campus has experienced the problem of low student motivation on low stakes standardized tests. In order to remedy this, some departments have established performance thresholds for their majors that are tied to advanced standing. If juniors do not achieve the minimum proficiency levels when they complete the general education examination, they may retake the test to improve their scores. If they have not met the requirement by the time they have completed 90 semester credit hours, they may not enroll in any major courses at the 300 level or higher. Since the proficiency scores are integrated throughout the examination, students cannot choose to work hard on small portions of the test, but must give it their best effort overall. The net result is that student proficiency scores increased dramatically for first-time test takers. Most students achieve the needed proficiency level in their first attempt; almost all do so by their second attempt.

As part of Step 3 of the Seven-Step Planning Process, each student service has developed a set of measures and indicators that are monitored on a short cycle. These measures are linked to the strategic service KQIs and to the area's tactical KQIs. As part of Step 5, baselines have been established and comparative performance data are collected. Better practices are systematically identified, at times through benchmarking, and performance goals set as improvements are initiated.

Steps 5 through 7 are the primary tools used to evaluate and improve programs and offerings. These require the collection of comparative data and performance goals to push the organization to higher levels of performance. Assessment results and course evaluations are used as a basis for improvement of programs and offerings. These data are presented and analyzed, and instructional improvements are determined on a regular basis at academic department meetings and department development days.

The Seven-Step Planning Process is a collaborative, iterative process. Following Step 7, the loop closes by identifying any corrective actions, and the process starts again so that improvements are continuous. In addition, the President's Cabinet, the Dean's Council, and the Strategic Planning Council meet frequently to implement process improvements and to discuss and broadcast the knowledge gained by units across the university.

Support Processes

Northwest's key support processes are an outgrowth of the university's mission and include campus safety, facilities, financial management, outsource partners, purchasing, communication and marketing, and human resources. Northwest uses its Seven-Step Planning Process to determine, design, and deliver support processes and to evaluate and improve them. Consistent with the approach used to establish process requirements for educational programs and student services, the process is used to ensure that input is received from and validated by student and stakeholder users of support processes.

Key support processes are designed using Steps 1 through 4 of the Seven-Step Planning Process. The service KQIs play an integral role in the determination of process requirements by providing a foundation for meeting customer expectations in the areas of people interaction, task productivity and accuracy, timeliness of response, safety concerns, communication elements, and attention given to customer suggestions. Specific training is provided to support staff personnel on how to apply the service KQIs.

Performance measures have been developed for all support processes. The unit KQIs may have multiple goals and critical success factors that use a variety of in-process and summative assessments, such as comment card feedback, bimonthly reports, focus groups with students and/or faculty, and weekly post-program monitoring. Continuous feedback and regular reporting provide improvement opportunities for performance teams. It is important to note that the Seven-Step Planning Process has been deployed to support service delivery partners, and that each partner designs, manages, and improves its processes using the Seven-Step Planning Process.

7

Western Wisconsin Technical College

Jerrilyn A. Brewer

Western Wisconsin Technical College (WWTC) was established in 1912 as the La Crosse Vocational School. Over the past 90 years, the institution has provided quality vocational education and training for area residents and has evolved into a comprehensive, publicly supported technical college committed to being the foremost provider of technical education and training for the region. WWTC serves approximately 21,000 students who are enrolled at the main campus in La Crosse or at one of six extended campuses located in western Wisconsin. There are 477 full-time employees. Six instructional divisions house all collegiate programs, including 40 associate degree programs, 19 technical diploma programs, and 4 certificates. The college also provides apprenticeship training, customized training, and technical assistance for business and industry. WWTC has invested considerable resources in the development of a virtual environment and offers both online courses and programs.

WWTC has been using the Baldrige criteria for quality since 1999 and has been recognized at the Mastery Level of the Wisconsin Forward Quality Award. The college was among the first schools selected to participate in the North Central Association Higher Learning Commission's Academic Quality Improvement Program (AQIP). WWTC has aligned its AQIP Action Projects with its four strategic priorities: enrollment, retention, student learning, and satisfaction.

Leadership Systems

Western Wisconsin Technical College (WWTC) operates under a shared governance model, with responsibilities balanced between the Local District Board and the State Board of the Wisconsin Technical College System (WTCS). As part of the Integrated Leadership System, WWTC senior leaders provide the vision for setting and deploying the college's values, short- and longer-term directions, and performance expectations. Members of the Senior Leadership Team include the president, vice president of instruction, vice president of college relations and student services, vice president of finance and operations, associate vice president of strategic effectiveness, and director of special services (see Figure 7.1).

Figure 7.1

The Leadership System at Western Wisconsin Technical College

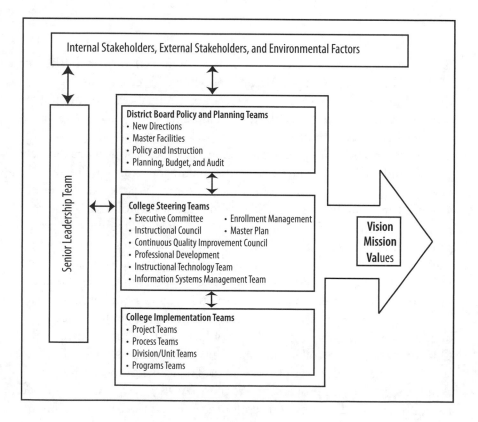

Senior leaders integrate college values into all aspects of operations. These values set forth the college's expectations regarding ethics, social responsibilities, community service, involvement, and a commitment to equity. Senior leaders set directions in alignment with the mission, vision, and values in a variety of ways. All decisions at the college are framed around achievement of the four strategic priorities—enrollment, retention, student learning, and satisfaction—thereby ensuring that the needs and expectations of students and key stakeholder groups are addressed. These priorities guide the development of strategic and annual plans.

Annual planning retreats that include the Senior Leadership Team and the District Board provide an opportunity to review the college's mission, vision, values, strategic priorities, and performance measures. Reports on progress in achieving these priorities are provided at monthly District Board meetings and at biweekly meetings of the college's Executive Committee. Senior leaders, union members, Instructional Council members, and a student representative all serve on this steering committee. The steering teams report either biweekly or monthly to the Executive Committee, thereby ensuring alignment with the mission, vision, and values. This reporting provides an opportunity for input, feedback, and collaborative decision-making on important issues.

In addition to the Integrated Leadership System, senior leaders communicate values, directions, and expectations to all employees by using a variety of written, oral, and electronic media. This provides for a constant flow of information throughout the college and multiple opportunities for faculty, staff, and students to interact with senior leaders formally and informally. Examples of communication efforts include budget forums held to keep employees informed of current budget challenges and Union/Management Forums held to inform employees of the new employment contracts prior to a ratification vote. Communication with extended campuses is enhanced by holding forums via interactive television.

Creating a Team Environment

WWTC employs a dynamic network of teams that connect the District Board, the Senior Leadership Team, the Steering Team, and the Implementation Team. These teams form the Integrated Leadership System and exemplify a commitment to collaborative decision-making. Additionally, this integrated team structure serves as the framework for ensuring that senior leaders communicate values, directions, and expectations to all faculty and staff.

District Board Teams set the direction for policy and planning decisions, thus ensuring a strong link between policy setting and implementation. Steering Teams play an important role in the leadership system by communicating values, directions, and expectations set forth in the strategic priorities. Implementation Teams reflect a college environment that promotes shared decision-making and staff involvement and provides the focus for creating and balancing value for students and stakeholders. Teams are cross functional and include staff from extended campuses. A variety of process, project, program, and division/unit teams engage in decision-making activities that ensure that the campus is making progress toward achieving the strategic priorities. The conceptual framework for decision-making is also the operational framework because decisions are made by people at the level where work is being done. This decision-making system is functional and is one of the strengths of the college. Employees at all levels are empowered to make decisions.

Leadership Development

Leadership abilities are encouraged, developed, and strengthened among faculty, staff, and administrators in a variety of ways. Senior leaders recommend individuals or seek recommendations from units that identify individuals to participate in formal local, state, and national leadership development activities based on an individual's perceived leadership potential, current involvement in the organization, and organizational needs. Examples of these formal leadership programs include the local Greater La Crosse Chamber of Commerce Leadership Program, the Wisconsin Leadership Development Institute (which is open to all employee groups), and the National Institute of Leadership Development.

The college also supports and encourages staff to pursue advanced degrees and has a tuition reimbursement policy that offsets the cost of tuition. On occasion, short-term professional development employment opportunities are available to employees that provide experience in a new job or role or expand individual knowledge and skills. These opportunities are often steppingstones to career progression and leadership roles in the organization. Thus, in offering both formal and in-house programs, the focus is on growing leaders from within the organization.

In June 2003, WWTC piloted a leadership institute, Leading and Learning Together, as one method to increase the breadth and depth of leadership opportunities across the college. The institute reiterated the focus on continuous improvement, systems thinking, performance excellence, and servant leadership. The institute was open to all interested managers, members of the Continuous Quality Improvement Council, past Wisconsin Leadership Development Institute participants, and individuals who participated in a training week leadership workshop. Forty-five staff members attended. The institute had the following objectives:

- Increase staff knowledge and understanding of various approaches to leadership

- Increase staff knowledge and understanding of the Baldrige performance excellence framework

- Increase staff knowledge and understanding of systems thinking

- Increase staff knowledge and ability to use appreciative inquiry as a communication and problem-solving tool

- Increase staff knowledge and ability to use conversation as a way to build collaborative relationships

- Provide staff an opportunity to reflect upon their own leadership style and to develop an Employee Success Plan that addresses leadership growth opportunities

Each of these areas was addressed during the two-day session that included a facilitator from the University of Wisconsin–Stout. A world café format was used to encourage sharing of ideas and collective thinking. This leadership institute was discussed at both the Continuous Quality Improvement Council and the Executive Committee, thus ensuring that faculty, staff, and administrators understood the importance of developing leadership capacity at the college.

WWTC's succession planning for leaders and board members promotes a process that ensures that the mission, vision, and values are passed on during leadership succession. Leaders planning retirement within a two- to three-year time period are encouraged to declare their retirement plans and to develop a transition plan that will shift some of their responsibilities to other people in the organization while the senior leader is actively employed. These individuals are then potential applicants for the position when it is posted.

Several measures of leadership and communication are collected and analyzed regularly.

- Formal leadership training participation

- A biennial modified version of the Personal Assessment of College Effectiveness (PACE) survey

- The Baldrige "Are We Making Progress?" survey (www.nist.gov)

- Informal staff feedback on the effectiveness of the "Coffee with the President" forums

An analysis of the Are We Making Progress? survey results and the development of the Leading and Learning Together Leadership Institute resulted in the college targeting three specific improvement priorities: 1) design and offer the second Leading and Learning Together Leadership Institute, 2) provide follow-up activities throughout the year for participants who attended the first Leadership Institute, and 3) administer the Are We Making Progress? survey on a college-wide basis.

Strategic Planning

WWTC's vision—"to be a collaborative, innovative educational leader in the community"—provides the context for setting strategic direction. To achieve this vision, WWTC addresses several strategic challenges.

- Provide a high-quality technical education with limited resources

- Align resources and services to support ever-changing needs and expectations of diverse student segments

- Align resources and services to support developmental needs of students

- Anticipate ever-changing needs and expectations of stakeholders

WWTC's mission—committed to excellence in learning, continuous improvement, student success, employer satisfaction, and responsiveness to the Western District—provides the context for planning and continuous improvement.

Strategic Planning Process

WWTC's Strategic Planning Process is dynamic and guides the college's programs and services, budget, and facilities planning on a five-year cycle (see Figure 7.2). This process enhances the ability to establish strategic priorities, addresses student and stakeholder needs, enhances performance relative to competitors, and improves overall performance. All aspects of the planning process are intended to broaden the college's ability to be responsive to the needs of the district.

Strategic priorities are identified for a five-year timeframe and provide focus on developing strategic plans for six key operational areas: 1) facilities, 2) technology, 3) instruction, 4) marketing, 5) enrollment, and 6) retention. Information from these plans is compiled into the five-year program and services, budget, and facilities document. An integral part of the Strategic Planning Process is the alignment of strategic challenges with strategic priorities to ensure that the priorities move forward with respect to WWTC's mission and vision. Mission, vision, strategic challenges, strategic priorities/objectives, Academic Quality Improvement Program (AQIP) Action Projects, key actions, performance measures, and targets are integrated into the Strategic Priorities Plan.

The Annual Program and Services, Budget, and Facilities Planning Process guides the yearly development of major division and unit-level action plans that include performance measures, resource needs, and budget implications. These annual plans direct the development of the subsequent year's budget. District Board members, senior leaders, administrators, faculty, and staff are all involved in this process throughout the various stages of planning and budget development. The Executive Com-

Figure 7.2

The Strategic Planning Process at Western Wisconsin Technical College

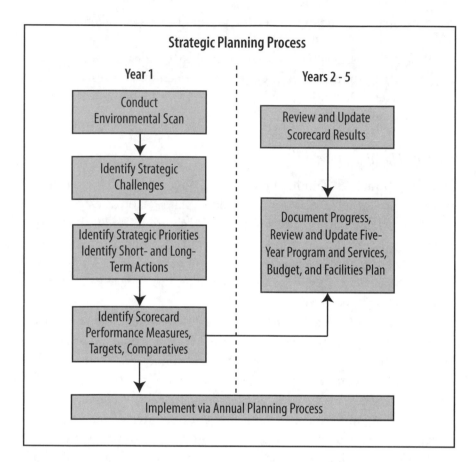

mittee provides the leadership for budget-related decisions as the subsequent year's budget is developed. This ongoing budget decision-making related to the division and unit-level action plans connects the planning and budgeting processes.

Action Plan Development

WWTC selects strategic priorities/strategies and related key short- and long-term actions by responding to the strategic challenges that impact the college. Action plan development occurs at both the college and major division/unit levels as part of the strategic and annual planning processes. Performance measures for the college-level strategic priorities and actions are tracked and analyzed over the five-year cycle and provide the framework for the WWTC scorecard and the basis for organizational performance review.

As part of the Annual Program and Services, Budget, and Facilities Planning Process, each major division/unit completes a planning workbook that includes a self-assessment of progress and an annual action plan with unit objectives, expected outcomes, timelines, resources needed (human, major equipment, minor equipment, supplies, and facilities), responsible person/unit, and total cost. These action plans are developed on a program-by-program basis in the instructional divisions and a department-by-department basis in the other units of the college.

Operational dollars are allocated as part of the budget development process. Capital equipment requests are funded separately and are allocated to units based on need and/or an internal allocation formula. As part of the planning process, the grants office works closely with units to identify new initiatives that might be supported by grant dollars. Funding sources are a key factor that significantly affects action plan development and deployment. Because of changes in state funding for the WTCS, WWTC must be as efficient as possible in resource utilization as evidenced by its low cost per student.

Key performance measures that track progress relative to action plans are identified in the Performance Measures column in the Strategic Priorities Plan. Progress reports for the college action plans are tracked and reviewed regularly at the bimonthly Executive Committee meetings, the monthly District Board meetings, and at the unit level. Progress is communicated to staff via meetings and electronic reports.

Aligning Strategic Planning Efforts Across the College

Aligning planning processes with overall institutional strategies occurs at the department and unit level through the development of short- and longer-term action plans. The alignment of these action plans with the strategic priorities and related performance measures ensures consistent deployment throughout the college and that faculty, staff, and administrators are working together to accomplish the strategic priorities.

WWTC selects measures and sets performance projections for institutional strategies and action plans partially through the use of common measures identified by the WTCS and the measures identified specifically to address progress related to the strategic priorities. Benchmarks from other higher education institutions, including schools that are members of the Continuous Quality Improvement Network and AQIP, are also reviewed during the planning process, and resource needs (i.e., staff, financial, facilities, technology, and equipment) are identified through budget development at the unit and department level. This information is used to create an institutional budget for the next year that is prioritized based upon college needs.

Continuous Improvement of Strategic Planning Processes

To measure the effectiveness of the college's systems for planning continuous improvement, WWTC utilizes strategic planning questions from the Malcolm Baldrige Are We Making Progress? Survey, the Wisconsin Forward and Baldrige award programs feedback reports relating to strategic planning, and feedback from the AQIP Systems Portfolio Review. The college improves processes and systems for planning continuous improvement by analyzing the Are We Making Progress? survey data, by soliciting informal feedback from employees about the effectiveness of the planning process, and by trending results of the modified PACE climate survey in the areas of organizational structure and work design. Analyses of these data indicated a need to improve planning through greater integration with the college's continuous quality improvement activities.

Specific improvement priorities to be addressed include more effective alignment of the planning process components with other college processes (i.e., program/services evaluation, continuous improvement, and information management.) Another focus area is continued improvement of the process for setting performance projections based on data analysis and competitor performance both inside and outside the WTSC. To address these improvements, the college created a new position—associate vice president for strategic effectiveness. This position has responsibility for implementing a new planning process, taking into account the concerns identified.

Students and Stakeholders

WWTC attracts a student population primarily from the 11 counties that comprise the district. The college segments its student groups to meet their needs more effectively. Current students are divided into eight key segments that are aligned with the WTCS Educational Aid Code Design. Associate degree, technical diploma, and certificate students are further segmented by academic programs within instructional divisions.

WWTC has both internal and external stakeholders. Employees are considered internal stakeholders; external stakeholders include alumni, employers, the community, District Board members, the WTCS, and local legislators. The short- and long-term requirements and expectations of the student and stakeholder groups are illustrated in Figure 7.3.

Understanding Student Needs

During the application and registration processes, future students supply the college with valuable information that is used for educational program and support service planning, marketing, and improvements. Students complete the ASSET/COMPASS entrance assessment test if they have not taken an ACT placement test or engaged in coursework at another postsecondary institution. These entrance tests assess students' skills in basic areas of reading, writing, and mathematics. Data from these assessment tests are analyzed to determine specific student needs and are used by student service advisors and counselors during the intake process to make decisions about the student's academic preparedness and to identify factors that could impact the student's ability to be successful. Student services has specialized support services in place to meet the needs of disabled, minority, international, academically disadvantaged, and nontraditional students; displaced homemakers; and dislocated workers.

After completing the registration/intake process, students are segmented by academic program and are assigned to a faculty advisor who works with them to provide scheduling and career information. Students are invited to participate in a new student orientation where they will receive general information regardless of the program selected. The intent is to help the students establish a connection early in their start at the college. Students can register online, by phone, or in person to attend one of the five three-hour orientation sessions that are scheduled prior to

Figure 7.3
Student and Stakeholder Requirements at Western Wisconsin Technical College

Students	Relationship-Building Mechanisms	Short- and Long-Term Requirements
Prospective Students • High school • Nontraditional	• High school visits • Surveys • On-site visits • Shopping mall kiosk • College web site	• Relevant, affordable, flexible, and accessible programs and courses
Current Students (8 Segments) • Associate degree • Technical diploma • General adult/occupational adult (non-degree) • Apprentices • Adult avocational • Adult basic education • Customized training clients • Certificate	• Focus groups • Student government • Surveys • Student organizations • Student newspaper • College web site • College publications • Faculty advisors	• Complete requirements to graduate, obtain employment, upgrade current skills

Stakeholders	Relationship-Building Mechanisms	Short- and Long-Term Requirements
Alumni	• Alumni database • Alumni newsletters • Alumni breakfasts • College Foundation	• Lifelong learning opportunities
Employers	• Employer follow-up survey • Focus groups • Advisory committees	• Well-trained employees
Community	• Town hall meetings • College web site • Newspaper, radio, and television	• Cost-effective education
District Board	• Board retreats • District Board meetings • Board/staff teams	• Fiscal responsibility to taxpayers
Wisconsin Technical College System	• State-called meetings • WTCS web site	• Adherence to Wisconsin State Statute 38.00 and WTCS policies
Local legislatures	• Public forums • Targeted meetings • Legislative staffers • Federal and state Legislative Days	• Enhance economic well-being of the community

the start of classes in the fall. In addition to the general college orientation, many of the divisions and programs conduct student orientation. These sessions provide information specific to the technical programs in which students are enrolled, identify student expectations, and provide the opportunity for students to ask questions about the program. Some programs offer a "job shadow" experience to help students learn more about the program prior to enrollment.

Currently enrolled students supply relevant information about their needs and expectations through the Noel-Levitz Student Satisfaction Inventory, student complaints/suggestions, student government, student course evaluations, formative student satisfaction surveys, and informal listening strategies. Student complaint feedback is important because it identifies systems or processes that may not be meeting student needs and expectations. Monthly meetings of student clubs and organizations also serve as effective listening and learning opportunities. A student government representative serves as a member of the College Executive Committee. Student evaluations of courses are designed to provide relevant data for instructors to use in improving their courses and program offerings.

Building Relationships With Students and Stakeholders

Prospective students have the opportunity to learn about the college and career offerings available on site at the La Crosse campus and at extended campus locations. The high school recruitment specialist visits area high schools regularly to meet with prospective students and high school counselors. Faculty also meet with students on campus and at local high schools to promote their programs. Relationships with nontraditional students occur through newspaper and television advertising, brochures, and semester schedules that are made available in public locations, at places of employment, and through collaboration with Wisconsin Job Service.

Student services and the instructional divisions are key areas in developing student relationships with current students. These relationships are established and maintained throughout students' academic careers from collaboration with the counselors, student services advisors, faculty, academic advisors, and staff. The relationships include classroom activities, student government involvement, student organizations, intramural and competitive athletic activities, work-study programs, free Wellness Center membership, student and family health care services, recognition of achievement in the student newspaper, and graduation ceremonies.

WWTC uses a variety of listening and learning strategies to gather relevant information that can be used to determine and anticipate changing stakeholder needs and expectations. A variety of listening and learning strategies is used to gather feedback from alumni, including graduate follow-up studies conducted at periodic intervals. Results from the Six-Month Graduate Follow-Up Survey and Five-Year Graduate Follow-Up Survey are used to develop future programs, plan for facilities, and design student support services that meet the ever-changing needs of students. For example, based on survey results, WWTC added more classes at the extended campuses and increased emphasis on developing more online courses and programs to meet the needs of currently employed adults who require additional education to advance in their careers.

Using Information From Students and Stakeholders

Although the WTCS broadly defines the student segments and/or markets the educational programs will address, each of Wisconsin's 16 technical colleges has the autonomy to offer programs to specifically meet the local needs of the community it serves. Thus, WWTC determines its specific market emphasis through student and employer research to determine new program course offerings. Since 1999, the college has implemented nine new programs and suspended six programs. As a result of changing needs, general use facilities were added to the Mauston campus, and a police firing range was built at the Sparta campus in partnership with Fort McCoy, a U.S. Army Reserve Training Center.

The college analyzes and selects a course of action regarding student needs by reviewing results of surveys, focus group sessions, and advisory committee input. Recently, WWTC analyzed program enrollments, cost per FTE, graduate placement, and graduate earnings in regard to overall efficiency. Comparative data from other technical colleges within the state that offer the same programs were also analyzed. As a result, the number of faculty was reduced in several programs, primarily through retirement or transfer to other areas of the college, and program offerings at one extended campus were reduced, one program was suspended, and a portion of a program was eliminated.

Measuring Institutional Effectiveness

WWTC uses a centralized data collection and retrieval system to collect and store information and data; discrete databases throughout the college feed into this centralized data warehouse. The data are made accessible to those who need them through a variety of different mechanisms (see Figure 7.4). PeopleSoft is a major component of the information management system.

Figure 7.4

Data Access Mechanisms at Western Wisconsin Technical College

User Groups	Information Needed	Access Mechanisms
Employees	• College policies and forms, human resources, predetermined reports (updated daily by management information systems), department web sites (i.e., human resources, research, division, or program), location for sharing all internal information of the college • State reporting information from state web sites	• WIRE—intranet web site for college employees
	• Administrative system for processing all campus information systems (i.e., admissions, registration, student finance, human resources/payroll, finance, student financial aid, Wisconsin state reporting, student and employee demographics)	• Legacy or PeopleSoft • Management information systems

User Groups	Information Needed	Access Mechanisms
	• All employees are expected to use the college-wide email/office management system, allowing for efficient communications and scheduling	• Email and active directory services
	• Public information for students and staff is available at www.wwtc.edu • Video conferencing between campuses and state locations	• College web site • Video conferencing— internal to the college and over the Internet
Students	• Course information and student support services, all public information available to students • Online courses along with web-enhanced face-to-face course information	• College public web site • College instructional web sites
	• Course information, graduate follow-up, student support services	• Brochures and catalogs
	• Courses and classes shared over ITV • Access to counseling with campus advisors from extended campus via video conferencing	• ITV and video conferencing
	• Register and access grades via touchtone phone	• Telephone registration system

continued on page 198

User Groups	Information Needed	Access Mechanisms
Community, Employers, District Board	• Comprehensive college updates and actions • Fiscal responsibility, graduation rate, graduation employment rate	• District Board meeting • WTCS web site • Brochures and annual report
Partners (K–12 and higher education)	• Online courses (Youth Options students) • Course articulation agreements • Tailored school-specific data • Fiscal responsibility, graduation rate, graduation employment rate	• College web site • High school linkage CD • WTCS web site
WTCS	• Client reporting and fiscal data meeting WTCS standardized criteria	• Quarterly Internet downloads, state and college web sites

The WWTC Scorecard

Key institutional measures for tracking effectiveness are identified in the WWTC scorecard. The framework for these measures is based upon the college strategic priorities—enrollment, retention, student learning, and satisfaction (see Figure 7.5).

The WTCS introduced a program scorecard that will continue to be used as part of the Quality Review Process for programs. The intent of this scorecard is to provide statewide comparative data for all instructional programs (see Figure 7.6).

Assessment of Student Learning Outcomes

WWTC is able to select, manage, and use information and data to support student learning by fully deploying an Assessment of Student Learning Program. Designed in 1995 and approved by the North Central Association's Higher Learning Commission, the college's Assessment Program guides this deployment in a well-defined, consistent manner. Entry-level

Figure 7.5
Key Institutional Measures for Tracking Effectiveness:
The Western Wisconsin Technical College Scorecard

Strategic Priority	Performance Measures	2002–2003 Results
Enrollment: Do We Get Them?	Total headcount/FTE	Headcount = 21,715 FTE = 3,768
	Extended campus headcount/FTE	Headcount = 9,062 FTE = 763
	Total alternative delivery headcount	6,849
	Cost per FTE	$10,440
	Fund balance (% of operating budget)	3.3%
	Graduates employed in district	79%
	Market share—high school graduates	32.8%
Retention: Do We Keep Them?	Cohort graduation rate	65.3%
	Graduate employment rate	95%
	Student satisfaction with college services	5.25 (7-pt. scale)
	Fall-to-spring retention (program declared)	81%
Student Learning: Do They Learn?	Developmental student success in credit courses	81.5%
	Student learning outcome achievement	97.2%
	GED pass rate	89%

continued on page 200

Strategic Priority	Performance Measures	2002–2003 Results
Satisfaction: Are Stakeholders Satisfied? (Student, Employee, and Stakeholder)	Employee success expenditures	$96,379
	Employee success plan implementation	165/479 (34%)
	Employee satisfaction with college environment	3.83 (5-pt. scale)
	Graduate satisfaction with training	97%
	Employer satisfaction with graduates' training	96%

assessments are conducted when students enter the college to determine appropriate placement into general education and/or developmental classes. Classroom-level assessments are conducted on an ongoing basis to monitor student learning in a formative manner. Exit-level assessments are conducted to measure student learning prior to graduation from a program.

WWTC's Exit-Level Assessment Program was cited by the Higher Learning Commission as a best practice in 2002. All instructional programs have clearly identified student-learning outcomes with criteria for assessment (these outcomes can be found on the college web site at www.wwtc.edu). Six general learning outcomes have been identified that all students are expected to master. Student learning data are collected electronically from faculty, students, and employers and are used by faculty to make improvements to instructional programs and curricula (student learning results are also available at www.wwtc.edu).

Using Comparative Data

The college seeks and uses key comparative data and information from within and outside academe to ensure effectiveness related to the stra-

Figure 7.6

The Wisconsin Technical College System Program Scorecard

Strategic Measure	Threshold Performance	Actual Performance*	Target Performance
State-Level Priorities (common reporting)	These threshold performance rates will be determined for all measures	*The performance for these measures will vary annually	Target performance for all measures will be determined
A) Course completion			
B) Special populations course completion			
C) Minority course completion			
D) Second-year retention			
E) Third-year retention			
F) Third-year graduation			
G) Fifth-year graduation			
H) Graduate placement rate, all employment			
I) Graduate placement rate, related employment			
J) Nontraditional gender enrollment			
College Priorities (each college creates up to 8 indicators)			
Program Priorities (each program has 1 to 2 indicators)			

tegic priorities, especially those making up the WWTC scorecard. Four types of comparative data are used: 1) internal, 2) state educational, such as the WTCS mean and best, 3) national educational, such as AQIP, Noel-Levitz, U.S. Department of Education Adult Education and Family Literacy indicators, and 4) national outside academe.

Internal data are trended to demonstrate progression toward achievement of key performance measures. State comparative performance indicators from the WTCS are used to demonstrate how the college is doing relative to its 15 sister colleges. National comparatives such as licensure exams and surveys demonstrate performance relative to other institutions of higher education. National comparatives outside academe help the organization determine effectiveness of organizational initiatives or processes. The methods and criteria used to select sources of comparative information vary depending upon the performance measure and what comparative information is available. For example, one of the reasons for selecting the Noel-Levitz Student Satisfaction with College Services Inventory is because comparative data are available. Figure 7.7 illustrates the variety of comparative performance measures used.

As baselines are established, data are collected and trended over a three- to five-year period for analysis. Targets and benchmarks (when available) are established for external comparisons. For example, national registry or licensure bodies publish national pass rates for exams, thus providing excellent program-specific comparative data. WWTC consistently scores above the national pass rates in many programs. Program teams utilize these measures to revise curriculum, demonstrate instructional effectiveness, and reflect student career preparedness.

Faculty and Staff

The distinctive ways in which WWTC organizes the work environment, work activities, and job classifications strengthen the college's focus on student learning and development. Work and jobs are designed and aligned primarily around work functions. Faculty, staff, and supervisors work collaboratively to ensure that strategic priorities are achieved and student and stakeholder needs are met. In addition, faculty positions are developed to meet the required educational design framework, and the workload is calculated in units that include both teaching and nonteaching activities.

Figure 7.7

Sample Comparative Information Used by Western Wisconsin Technical College

Comparison	Comparative/Benchmarking Partner
Licensure exam pass rate	American Registry of Radiological Technologists
Graduate employment rate	WTCS
Student satisfaction with services	Noel-Levitz
Employer satisfaction with graduates	*Measuring Up 2000*
Cost per FTE	WTCS
Employee satisfaction with college environment	Personal Assessment of College Environment (PACE)
Employee turnover rate	AQIP Consortium
Are We Making Progress? Survey	Baldrige National Quality Program

The highly integrated, cross-functional system of standing committees, steering teams, and project and process teams forms the foundation for the college's work processes and activities. This system encourages shared decision-making and collaborative problem solving, thereby enhancing communication, cooperation, organizational learning, and skill sharing. Teams serve as a means of communication, interaction, and formal and informal staff knowledge/skill sharing across departments, jobs, and locations, and provide the framework for strengthening employee-based decision-making at all levels. This team structure also offers opportunities for campus-wide input on work processes.

Employee unions are a key part of the work system. Faculty and staff are organized formally and represented by the Western Wisconsin Federation of Employees Local 3605; the Teamsters Local 695 represents the custodial staff, including maintenance staff. Faculty and staff provide input on job design, compensation, and recognition by participating in monthly union meetings and union contract negotiations, and three members represent Local 3605 on the Executive Committee. Local 3605 represents full- and part-time contract faculty, nonteaching professional, and paraprofessional and school-related personnel. Members from these employee groups represent Local 3605 on key college steering and implementation teams. The Federation bargains with the local District Board on wages, hours, workloads, and working conditions, and also represents the members of their respective units when complaints arise.

The Hiring Process

Broadly speaking, WWTC identifies specific credentials, skills, and values required for faculty, staff, and administrators by carefully reviewing, revising, and updating all open positions that occur at the college prior to posting positions, either internally or externally. With the rapid turnover of staff due to retirements, the college had the unique opportunity to review job descriptions to ensure they adequately reflected the specific skills and credentials required for the positions and the institutional values. During the interview process, information is sought to help selection committees determine if the person being interviewed reflects appropriate values in his or her statements.

Beginning at the unit level, managers identify characteristics and skills needed by potential employees. Faculty skills and characteristics are determined by certification requirements defined by the WTCS education design code. Managers closely examine each vacancy in terms of its function to determine if the position can be restructured, redesigned, or eliminated to effectively meet emerging college needs. On an ongoing basis, the Executive Committee reviews the open-positions report to plan for the replacement of retiring employees and positions that become open due to resignations. Each position is reviewed to make one of four determinations: 1) if the position needs to be filled immediately or if it can be held open for a time, thus allowing a temporary salary savings, 2) if the position can be filled by a temporary replacement, 3) if the position can be combined with one or more existing positions, or 4) if the position can be eliminated.

WWTC ensures that the people it employs possess the requisite characteristics through the use of a hiring matrix. Based upon an evaluation of the hiring process in June 1999, a project team was formed to develop a hiring process matrix for each employee group. The matrix was developed to establish legal compliance with statutory and college selection requirements while striving to employ the best-qualified candidate for the position. The human resources department serves as a resource to each unit/selection committee throughout the hiring process.

In addition to full-time faculty members, WWTC uses adjunct faculty for teaching both credit and noncredit courses. A database of approximately 400 adjunct faculty members is maintained, and approximately 200 instructors teach part-time each semester. The adjunct faculty who teach credit courses must meet the same certification requirements as full-time faculty. An adjunct faculty handbook provides these part-time employees with information about the college and access to needed resources.

WWTC relies on employment services to provide a pool of qualified individuals for temporary custodial and office support positions. In addition, Riverfront, Inc., a facility that places and trains developmentally disabled adults, is a source of part-time help for the cafeteria. Additionally, students funded through the federal work-study program provide flexible, part-time employment in a variety of positions throughout the college.

Employee Training and Development

As the college reviews workforce needs for the next decade, the following demographic trends will be considered: 1) rapid increase in turnover of faculty and staff who are nearing retirement, 2) emerging technology that will impact the program offerings and require faculty and staff to acquire specialized skills, 3) emerging occupations that may require new program offerings and retraining of current staff or hiring new staff, and 4) the decline in existing occupations that may affect current program offerings. All of these trends and factors will have significant implications for employee training and development.

The college is developing plans to implement key faculty, staff, and administrative training initiatives.

• Course management system training and refresher training

• Software training (ongoing monthly training sessions)

• LEAN manufacturing training

- Leadership

- PeopleSoft

- Various instructional technology workshops

- Worldwide Instructional Design Software curriculum development

- Conflict resolution

- Consensus decision-making

- Appreciative inquiry

Three weeks are set aside during each academic year as training weeks. Training offerings are varied based on interest and need and are open to all employees. New staff members participate in a one-day orientation session and a one-day training session, "Becoming a Great College," that focuses on the college's continuous improvement philosophy, processes, and role in contributing to the four strategic priorities. Additionally, all new faculty attend a two-day new faculty institute. Cross-functional teams composed of individuals throughout the college provide training for these activities. New faculty members also participate in a one-year mentor program. Mentors are trained in faculty coaching, mentoring techniques, analyses of classroom scenarios, and basics of effective teaching.

Faculty and staff evaluate training and professional activities using formal and informal processes (e.g., written evaluations and verbal feedback.) These results, coupled with results from needs surveys and the PACE climate survey, provide data that are analyzed and used by the human resources department, the Professional Development Steering Team, and the Executive Committee to improve education and training offerings that align with strategic priorities.

Employee Success Policy

WWTC's Employee Success Policy serves as an alternative to the traditional employee performance appraisal process. This policy is an approach to human resource development that emphasizes the inherent ability of every employee to grow and succeed. The employee success concept is based on the theories of W. Edwards Deming and others who contend that 95% of all employees are working for organizational success and only 5% of all employees are experiencing serious difficulties. There are three components to the Employee Success Policy: the Employee Success Plan, the Probationary Performance Appraisal, and the Special Performance Appraisal.

Each employee at the college is responsible for developing an Employee Success Plan that must align an individual's professional and personal goals with division/unit goals, as well as with overall organizational goals to support high performance and a student/stakeholder focus. Each plan is reviewed annually in a joint dialogue with the supervisor and is intended to focus on employee improvement through positive support for the employee and encouragement by the supervisor. The Employee Success Plan provides a vehicle for ongoing employee/supervisor dialogue and creates an environment of encouragement, trust, and mutual commitment.

The Probationary Performance Appraisal is used for new employees to assist them in adapting to their work environment. Once the employee has successfully completed the probationary period, the employee will develop an Employee Success Plan and does not undergo an annual performance review. The Special Performance Appraisal is used for the 5% of employees who may be struggling in performance. The appraisal is developed with the immediate supervisor and offers specific directions and a timeline for improvement. It also includes specific consequences if poor performance continues. The power of the Special Performance Appraisal exists in the combined message of support from the supervisor coupled with very real consequences for noncompliance in meeting agreed-upon goals. Once the employee has successfully completed the special appraisal, he or she will return to using the Employee Success Plan as the tool for growth and improvement.

Academic Program Management

Wisconsin state statutes define the mission and purpose of the WTCS, which is the governing body of the 16 technical college districts within the state. The mission of establishing less than baccalaureate level, postsecondary educational opportunities is a shared responsibility between the WTCS Board and the college, resulting in an educational design process that is multifaceted and well defined by the WTCS Board.

WWTC's offerings include 40 associate of applied science degree programs, 19 technical diploma programs, and 4 certificates. The college also offers apprenticeship training, noncredit courses, and customized training and technical assistance for business and industry. Adult Basic Education includes developmental education, remedial education, English for Speakers of Other Languages, High School Credential (or regular high school diploma), High School Equivalency Diploma, and General Educational Development Certificate.

Sharing programs with other colleges within the technical college system continues to increase, thus reducing the cost of maintaining complete programs. Examples of such program delivery include the associate degrees in dental hygiene and in fire protection technician and the technical diploma in pharmacy technician. As a result of a state-wide shared curriculum effort, the associate degrees in paralegal and supervisory management are now offered online as well as in traditional format. The supervisory management program has been successfully offered in an accelerated format, where students attend classes as a cohort group to complete an associate degree in 18 months.

Design of New Programs and Courses

WWTC designs new programs and courses to facilitate student learning using the New Program Development Process described in Figure 7.8. The process is comprehensive, and each step requires approval by the WTCS Board.

All instructors use the WIDS (Worldwide Instructional Design Software) curriculum development model to develop course outcome summaries that identify course goals, competencies, criteria, and learning activities. Each program curriculum is available via the college catalog and posted on the college web site. Course outcome summaries for courses developed using WIDS are available at the program web site, and faculty can develop course syllabi, lesson plans, learning plans, and rubrics utilizing this software.

Incorporating Technology Into Program and Course Design

New technology is incorporated into programs and courses based on program needs identified in the initial program development or subsequent curriculum modification and available funds. These changing needs are

Figure 7.8
The Academic Program Design Process at Western Wisconsin Technical College

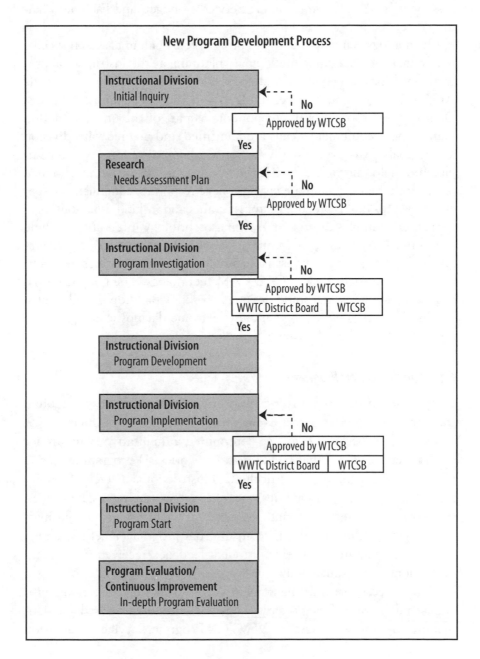

identified through student feedback, advisory committee input, focus groups, feedback obtained by faculty at internship/clinical site visits, employer satisfaction surveys, formal Program/Services Evaluation process, and the Annual Program and Services, Budget, and Facilities Planning Process.

Technology is incorporated into program curriculum based on specific requirements of the discipline. Primary planning at the instructional program level for both equipment and technology takes place as part of the Annual Program and Services, Budget, and Facilities Planning Process. Divisions incorporate both components as part of the one-year action plans, where equipment needs are identified and aligned with division action goals. A two-year hardware/software appraisal form is also completed to help inform the district-wide Technology Plan. Although much of this technology is purchased using college resources, equipment for specific programs is also procured through grants and in-kind donations.

Other examples of program-specific technology integration include electronic instruments used in human services programs such as radiography and police science. Industrial technology programs such as mechanical design use sophisticated CAD/CAM technology. The graphic design program added a photo stand designed to shoot tabletop digital photographs. The automotive program uses electronic diagnostic equipment to provide state-of-the-art training opportunities.

Evaluating Academic Programs

WWTC monitors the currency and effectiveness of the curriculum through the Program/Services Evaluation Process illustrated in Figure 7.9. Within that process, the college determined a qualitative structure for program effectiveness that includes six categories: 1) program team and administrative planning, 2) curriculum, 3) instructional delivery, 4) equipment and resources, 5) facilities, and 6) linkages (advisory committees, support services, secondary and postsecondary institutions, and business and industry). Ongoing efforts to ensure that programs meet key design and delivery requirements rely on student feedback received from course evaluations and graduate follow-up surveys.

This process serves as the framework for evaluating educational programs and offerings. The primary goal is to facilitate data-based decision-making to improve programs. WWTC's Program/Services Evaluation

Figure 7.9

The Evaluation Process for Programs and Services at Western Wisconsin Technical College

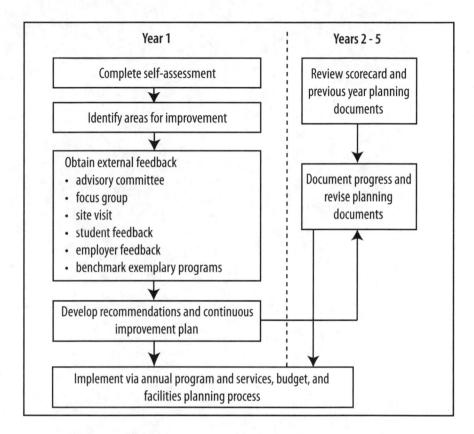

Process adheres to guidelines set forth by the WTCS for evaluation of programs and services. Educational programs and services are evaluated on
a rotating, five-year cycle. Approximately 10 to 12 programs and service
units are evaluated each year. Evaluation activities are conducted using
the Continuous Improvement Model and the PLAN (Developing a Plan),
DO (Implementing the Plan), CHECK (Data Gathering), ACT (Analysis
and Decision-Making) cycle. The Program/Services Evaluation Process
integrates evaluation activities with existing college initiatives and operational procedures.

8

Lessons Learned

As with any new quality or management system, the path is not always smooth as an organization assimilates new processes. Especially in higher education, it seems there is a need to discuss, debate, and deliberate the merits of any proposed change. And it was no different for the six institutions highlighted in this book. The Baldrige National Quality Award program criteria were questioned, the performance of award recipients was analyzed, and the rights of faculty were emphasized. Faculty and staff fell into the traditional groups of early adopters, wait-and-see, and over my dead body. As these six organizations persisted and committed to improved performance through the implementation of the Baldrige National Quality Program, eight lessons emerged.

1) Leadership: Can Passion for Quality Substitute for Leadership Commitment?

The experiences of the organizations in this book indicate leadership commitment is absolutely essential. Numerous higher educational institutions have established offices of quality and continuous improvement. Organizationally, they are located at different levels within institutions, but their purpose is singular—to improve the performance of the organization utilizing recognized tools and systems of continuous improvement. The success of these offices is checkered and is entirely dependent on the buy-in and support of individual departments and frontline leaders.

The evidence from the six institutions reflects the necessity of stable senior leadership coupled with commitment and active involvement from leaders at every level in the organization, including governance.

Successful leadership means shared responsibility and accountability. It also requires reflection on the organization's leadership system—does the leadership system align with the quality values of participation, informed decision-making, and communication? The Baldrige model, applied with commitment over time, results in a leadership environment that fosters empowerment, innovation, and a shared vision among faculty, staff, and senior leaders.

2) Systems: Can Organizational Silos Be Eliminated?

The Baldrige National Quality Award program is a powerful management system because it challenges organizations to identify and recognize existing systems within their organization. Systems encompass every aspect of any organization from student recruitment to delivery of instruction, from planning to human resource management. Once systems are documented, work can begin in continuous improvement on an organization-wide scale.

Organizational silos typically prevent collaboration and communication, isolate inhabitants from the larger organization, and produce competitive tendencies. The six institutions all continue to have traditional organization structures but have found methods to align organizational behavior with the Baldrige criteria. These methods encompass overarching leadership teams or councils, formal team building and professional development programs, rewards and recognition aligned with the Baldrige criteria, and a methodical approach for deploying the Baldrige criteria.

3) Clarity: Who Are Our Stakeholders? What Do They Want?

For decades, higher education organizations have been generally nonchalant about addressing the needs of students and stakeholders. Many were unsure what the word contextually meant; others were sure they already knew what was best for their students. Since the 1950s, there has been tremendous growth in college enrollments, faculty, staff, and facilities. Generous funding from public and private sources has allowed for the development of new academic programs while maintaining low tuition levels. The population growth resulting from the baby boomers and most recently from the echo-boomers continues the belief within the academy that higher education must continue to be a priority for funding. With increasing enrollments and little accountability, there have been few compelling reasons for most colleges and universities to systematically determine and satisfy the needs of their students and stakeholders.

However, for many institutions, both public and private, there is an increased awareness and trepidation regarding the cost of higher education, the permanent decline in tax-dollar support, and expectations from all sectors for accountability. The six institutions studied utilize the Baldrige criteria to determine requirements, expectations, and preferences of students, stakeholders, and markets. The institutions understand the importance of developing successful relationships with students and stakeholders and continued satisfaction with programs and services in all sectors of the organization that leads to improved retention and graduation. Each of the institutions utilizes market and student data with segmentation to design and improve programs and services. These organizations are able to align programs and services with the organizational vision and mission, demonstrating the ability to avoid waste of resources.

4) Change: Just Do It, But How?

Institutions utilizing the Baldrige criteria are characterized as agile, meeting the emerging needs of stakeholders and students. While this is challenging in higher education, change is possible, and utilizing the Baldrige criteria allows change to occur rapidly. This can happen in two very different ways. First, institutions that apply to a quality award program, either at the state or national level, commit to an elevated rate of change. The feedback reports provided through these programs present opportunities for improvement, thus encouraging notable progress in each application cycle.

Second, and more important, deploying the Baldrige criteria requires a planning system that aligns actions with the organization's values, vision, and mission, ensuring responsiveness to stakeholder needs. Using the criteria requires ongoing attention to outcomes through the identification of performance indicators. And, as the six institutions demonstrated, adopting the Baldrige values of organizational learning, focusing on the future, managing for innovation, and valuing faculty, staff, and partners creates an environment of trust and openness to change.

5) Data: Why Accept the Challenge to Look Outside of Your Organization?

All institutions have data and use data—fact books, financial reports, various surveys, and other reports are common. What makes the institutions using the Baldrige criteria distinctive is their quest to utilize data trends and segments, benchmark against competitors and peers, identify best-in-class organizations, and, importantly, benchmark outside of higher education. Further, these institutions utilize this data in continuous improvement initiatives, as well as to guide planning and resource allocation decisions.

Similar to business and industry, challenges in expanding data usage exist. Common data definitions, access to data, and appropriate use of data continue to be problematic. The six institutions suggest several benchmarking methods.

- Use of national data sets and reports such as *Measuring Up*

- Participation in commercial benchmarking studies that provide data beyond average and median

- Partnerships with noneducation sector organizations to share best-in-class systems for leadership, complaint management, and safety

- Utilization of increasingly sophisticated and available web data

This type of data use requires an institutional commitment to research and analysis, but the payoff is significant. Benchmarking is one of the most effective antidotes to complacency—a stigma that higher education currently carries. Business and industry clearly understands the need for reinvention and revitalization. Higher education continues to dismiss the for-profit education companies as a fad, although their growth and profit rates are spiking. Benchmarking provides every institution a tool to remain competitive.

6) Assessment: Will We Ever Be Ready to Apply for a Quality Award?

Perfectionists need not apply! The most common remark heard from organizations that have visited the University of Wisconsin–Stout is that they are reluctant to apply to an award program because too much improvement needs to take place first. In fact, the exact opposite is true. Each of the institutions in this book submitted its self-assessment application for review and scoring through a state quality award program or to the Malcolm Baldrige National Quality Award program. As a result, they received high-quality feedback from experienced examiners and were able to use the information to move their institution to an even higher level.

The feedback reports are typically in the format of identifying areas of strengths and opportunities for improvement in each of the criteria categories. The identification of strengths validates institutional efforts and motivates organization employees to accelerate implementation efforts. The opportunities for improvement also provide motivation—to deal with a problem that has existed for years or to develop expertise in an area where a void was identified. Although each institution received some form of recognition for its efforts, the prospect of an award does not drive these institutions; instead, it is the desire for continuous improvement.

7) Strengths: Do We Need to Start From Scratch?

These stories from six institutions demonstrate six different approaches to utilizing the Baldrige criteria. The criteria are nonprescriptive and easily applied to all types of higher education institutions: public, private, for-profit, two-year, four-year, highly-selective, and open access. The Baldrige criteria indicate that the same seven-part framework can be used for the education category as is used in the business and health care categories. There is great flexibility and adaptability between types of organizations. This is good news because each institution can determine the extent and depth to initially infuse the Baldrige criteria and can build on the existing inventory of institutional strengths. Participants in the award programs clearly understand that the journey is not over once an award is received. Rather the award initiates the challenge that the institution has the ability to achieve even greater outcomes.

8) Organizational Learning: What Is in It for Me?

The six institutions convey that implementation of the Baldrige criteria or any comprehensive quality program is hard work—it requires commitment and resources. It also provides an unequaled opportunity for organizational and personal learning. Senior leaders are able to model an effective management and continuous improvement system to other employees within their organization, one that is easily emulated at all levels and applies to almost any operation. The Baldrige approach transfers from sector to sector—education to business—making partnerships and communication more effective and rewarding. Faculty can choose to integrate Baldrige criteria into classroom settings, providing graduates with one more skill set to add to their repertoire. Individuals can participate at the state or national level as examiners, providing easy access to best practices nationwide.

Looking Into the Future

"Business as usual" really means challenge and change. Whether your educational challenges are the diverse needs of your students, the Internet and alternative educational services, accreditation, school transitions, facility management, rapid innovation, performance to budget, or maintaining your competitive advantage within the education community, the Baldrige Education Criteria can help you address them.

This statement from the Baldrige National Quality Program application demonstrates the inclusiveness and effectiveness of the model. The criteria easily accommodate other quality tools already in place at an institution or provide the foundation when an institution makes a commitment to performance excellence. Indeed, a major strength of the Baldrige criteria is its comprehensive approach—something lacking in most quality systems. Fully deployed, the criteria cover every aspect of an institution.

As indicated by the six institutions, this comprehensive approach is a new direction for higher education and demonstrates that quality management system tools are effective in any size or type of organization. The institutions demonstrate breakthrough change—significant and steady progress toward performance goals. Further, it is believed that the Baldrige approach will penetrate higher education quickly due to its adoption by higher education boards composed in part of successful business leaders. As accreditation agencies migrate toward a forward-looking accreditation process that provides the public with credible quality assurance, the Baldrige model will become increasingly important for institutions seeking or maintaining accreditation.

The Malcolm Baldrige National Quality Award criteria provide a simple but effective solution to address the unprecedented challenges faced by all higher education institutions. Are you ready?

Resources for Quality Improvement in Higher Education

State and National Quality Award Programs

Baldrige National Quality Program
www.quality.nist.gov
Phone: 301-975-2036

Baldrige National Quality Program
NIST
100 Bureau Drive Stop 1020
Gaithersburg, MD 20899-1020

California Council for Excellence
www.calexcellence.org/cce/home
Phone: 858-486-0400

California Council for Excellence
PO Box 1235
Poway, CA 92074-1235

Colorado Performance Excellence
www.coloradoexcellence.org
Phone: 303-893-2739

Colorado Performance Excellence
700 North Colorado Blvd
Suite 354
Denver, CO 80206

Missouri Quality Award
www.mqa.org/qualityaward.htm
Phone: 573-526-1725

Excellence in Missouri Foundation
205 Jefferson Street, 14th Floor
PO Box 1085
Jefferson City, MO 65102

Quality New Mexico
www.qualitynewmexico.org
Phone: 505-944-2001

Quality New Mexico
PO Box 25005
Albuquerque, NM 87102

Wisconsin Forward Award
www.forwardaward.org
Phone: 608-663-5300

Wisconsin Forward Award, Inc.
2909 Landmark Place, Suite 110
Madison, WI 53713

Featured Schools

Kenneth W. Monfort
College of Business,
University of Northern Colorado
www.mcb.unco.edu
Phone: 970-351-2764

Kenneth W. Monfort
College of Business
University of Northern Colorado
Kepner 2053, Campus Box 128
Greeley, CO 80639

National University
www.nu.edu
Phone: 858-642-8000

National University
11255 North Torrey Pines Road
La Jolla, CA 92037

New Mexico State
University–Carlsbad
www.cavern.nmsu.edu
Phone: 505-234-9200

New Mexico State
University–Carlsbad
1500 University Drive
Carlsbad, NM 88220

Northwest Missouri State University
www.nwmissouri.edu
Phone: 800-633-1175

Northwest Missouri
State University
800 University Drive
Maryville, MO 64468

University of Wisconsin–Stout
www.uwstout.edu
www.uwstout.edu/mba (Center for Assessment and Continuous Improvement)
www.uwstout.edu/bpa (Budget, Planning, and Analysis)
Phone: 715-232-5901

University of Wisconsin–Stout
One Clock Tower Plaza
325 Administration Building
Menomonie, WI 54751

Western Wisconsin Technical College
www.western.tec.wi.us
Phone: 800-248-9982

Western Wisconsin
Technical College
304 6th Street North
La Crosse, WI 54601

Testing and Survey Resources

ACT
(Student Opinion Survey, Alumni Outcomes Survey, Collegiate Assessment of Academic Proficiency, Adult Learners Needs Assessment, Enrollment Information Service)
www.act.org
Phone: 319-337-1000

ACT
500 ACT Drive
PO Box 168
Iowa City, IA 52243-0168

ASSET/COMPASS
Entrance Assessments
ASSET Student Success System
www.act.org/asset
COMPASS/ESL System
www.act.org/compass
Phone: 319-337-1000

ACT
500 ACT Drive
PO Box 168
Iowa City, IA 52243-0168

Baldrige National Quality Program
Are We Making Progress?
Baldrige Survey
www.quality.nist.gov/Progress.htm
Phone: 301-975-2036

Baldrige National Quality Program
NIST
100 Bureau Drive Stop 1020
Gaithersburg, MD 20899-1020

Educational Testing Service (ETS)
www.ets.org
Phone: 609-921-9000

Educational Testing Service
Rosedale Road
Princeton, NJ 08541

National Survey of
Student Engagement
www.indiana.edu/~nsse
Phone: 812-856-5824

National Survey of Student
Engagement
Center for Postsecondary Research
Indiana University Bloomington
Eigenmann Hall, Suite 419
1900 East Tenth Street
Bloomington, IN 47406-7512

Noel-Levitz Student
Satisfaction Inventory
www.noellevitz.com/solutions/
retention/satisfaction/ssi/index.asp
Phone: 800-876-1117

Noel-Levitz
2101 ACT Circle
Iowa City, IA 52245

Personal Assessment of
College Environment (PACE)
www.ced.ncsu.edu/acce/
nilie/surveys.html
Phone: 919-515-8567

National Initiative for Leadership
& Institutional Effectiveness
North Carolina State University
College of Education
300 Poe Hall, Box 7801
Raleigh, NC 27697-7801

Watson Wyatt Data Services
www.wwdssurveys.com
Phone: 201-843-1177

Watson Wyatt Data Services
218 Route 17 North
Rochelle Park, NJ 07662

Comparative Data and Benchmarking Resources

American Productivity and
Quality Center (APQC)
www.apqc.org
Phone: 800-776-9676

APQC
123 N. Post Oak Lane, Third Floor
Houston, TX 77024

College and University
Personnel Association for Human
Resources (CUPA-HR)
www.cupahr.org
Phone: 865-637-7673

CUPA-HR
Tyson Place
2607 Kingston Pike, Suite 250
Knoxville, TN 37919

Consortium for Student
Retention Data Exchange (CSRDE)
http://tel.occe.ou.edu/csrde
Phone: 405-325-2158

Consortium for Student Retention
Data Exchange
1700 Asp Avenue
Norman, OK 73072

Educational
Benchmarking, Inc. (EBI)
www.webebi.com
Phone: 417-831-1810

EBI Service Center
1630 W. Elfindale
Springfield, MO 54807

Integrated Postsecondary
Education Data System (IPEDS)
www.nces.ed.gov/ipeds
Phone: 202-502-7300

National Center for
Education Statistics
1990 K Street, NW
Washington, DC 20006

Measuring Up 2002
http://measuringup.highereduca
tion.org/2002/reporthome.htm
Phone: 408-271-2699

The National Center for Public
Policy and Higher Education
152 North Third Street, Suite 705
San Jose, CA 95112

National Center for
Education Statistics (NCES)
www.nces.ed.gov
Phone: 202-502-7300

National Center for
Education Statistics
1990 K Street, NW
Washington, DC 20006

Professional Organizations and Conferences

American Association of State Colleges and Universities (AASCU)
www.aascu.org
Phone: 202-293-7070

American Association of State
Colleges and Universities
1307 New York Avenue, NW
Washington, DC 20005

Continuous Quality Improvement Network (CQIN)
www.cqin.org
Phone: 707-746-7484

Staff Administrator
Continuous Quality Improvement
Network
335 St. Augustine Ct.
Benicia, CA 94510

National Association of College and University Business Officers (NACUBO)
www.nacubo.org
Phone: 202-861-2500

National Association of College
and University Business Officers
2501 M Street, NW, Suite 400
Washington, DC 20037

National Consortium for Continuous Improvement in Higher Education (NCCI)
www.ncci-cu.org
Phone: 202-861-2500
or 914-276-2717

NCCI Administrative Coordinator
NACUBO
2501 M Street, NW, Suite 400
Washington, DC 20037-1308

Quest for Excellence Conference
www.quality.nist.gov/Quest_
for_Excellence.htm
Phone: 301-975-2036

Baldrige National Quality Program
NIST
100 Bureau Drive Stop 1020
Gaithersburg, MD 20899-1020

Regional Accreditation Associations

Academic Quality Improvement Program (AQIP)
www.aqip.org
Phone: 800-621-7440

Higher Learning Commission
30 N. LaSalle Street, Suite 2400
Chicago, IL 60602-2504

Southern Association of Colleges and Schools
www.sacs.org
Phone: 404-679-4500

Southern Association of
Colleges and Schools
1866 Southern Lane
Decatur, GA 30033

*Western Association of
Schools and Colleges*
www.wascweb.org

Senior College Commission
www.wascweb.org/senior
Phone: 510-748-9001

Western Association of
Schools and Colleges
985 Atlantic Avenue, Suite 100
Alameda, CA 94501

Accrediting Commission for
Community and Junior Colleges
www.accjc.org
Phone: 415-506-0234

Accrediting Commission for
Community and Junior Colleges
10 Commercial Boulevard
Novato, CA 94949

Index